THE OWL AND THE WOODPECKER

THE OWL

AND THE

WOODPECKER

Encounters with North
America's Most Iconic Birds

PAUL BANNICK

FOREWORD BY TONY ANGELL
AUDIO RECORDINGS BY MARTYN STEWART

THE MOUNTAINEERS BOOKS

THE MOUNTAINEERS BOOKS
is the nonprofit publishing arm of The Mountaineers Club, an organization founded in 1906 and dedicated to the exploration, preservation, and enjoyment of outdoor and wilderness areas.

1001 SW Klickitat Way, Suite 201, Seattle, WA 98134

© 2008 by Paul Bannick

Foreword © 2008 by Tony Angell
Audio recordings © 2008 by Martyn Stewart/NatureSound.org

First edition, 2008

Manufactured in China

Copy Editor: Heath Lynn Silberfeld / enough said
Book Design: Mayumi Thompson
Cartographer: Ben Pease
All photographs by the author.

Cover photograph: *A Northern Hawk-Owl perches on a frosted branch between dawn hunts in the boreal forest.*
Frontispiece: *A male Snowy Owl glides back to the nest with a lemming on an Arctic summer night.*
Backcover: *An Acorn Woodpecker lands briefly before continuing his efforts to drive a squirrel from his granary.*

Library of Congress Cataloging-in-Publication Data
Bannick, Paul, 1963-
 The owl and the woodpecker : encounters with North America's most iconic birds / Paul Bannick. — 1st ed.
     p. cm.
 Includes bibliographical references and index.
 ISBN-13: 978-1-59485-095-0
 ISBN-10: 1-59485-095-X
 1. Owls—North America. 2. Woodpeckers—North America. I. Title.
QL696.S8B36 2008
598.9'7097—dc22
                          2008005366

To my late father, William R. Bannick, a writer, who shared his passion for photography with me and whose twenty-five years of volunteer coaching of children served as an example of giving back to the community

And to my mother, Mary Anne Bannick, who generously nurtured the unique interests of each of her thirteen children, including my own passion for birds and the rest of the natural world

Contents

Opposite: An Acorn Woodpecker retrieves an acorn from a nest cavity before fitting it into one of the vacant holes in a granary.

Foreword

Nature has always defined human character and directed our purposes. Among our first civilized efforts were creative expressions, using the materials at hand, that recorded our responses to the great mammals and birds we shared the world with. For thousands of generations we mythically celebrated their form, strength, and spirit as paintings on the walls of caves and in carvings of bone and stone. It wasn't, however, until five hundred years ago that we began to look more objectively at what we observed around us. Ships exploring new worlds then started including artists as part of their crews. With varying skill they sketched some of the exotic flora and fauna encountered. These early efforts initiated a process whereby information combined with aesthetics to expand understanding and to clarify what was newly discovered. This legacy of interpretation and celebration of nature continues to this day.

A hundred and fifty years ago, photography began to influence our perception of the world, but it wasn't until the beginning of the twentieth century that an earnest attempt was made to record North America's natural heritage. By that time the age of the great natural history illustrators was passing and photographers were lugging their ponderous box cameras into alpine meadows, deep forests, swamps, and canyons to photograph the wildlife residing there. Most of the resulting pictures showed distant and undistinguished subjects. Over the past half century, however, technology has made a vast difference in how we see the world. Telephoto lenses, remote triggers, fast film, and digital systems, to name a few innovations, allow the photographer to enter into the life of the wild as never before, at a level far more intimate than can be achieved with the naked eye. Fascinating and instructive as this access can be, it can distract us sometimes with its detail and scale from the more important and subtle stories to be told. Rather than seeing the fullness of an animal's habitat—its behavior, and its relationship to the community around it—we are left only with detailed impressions of feathers and fur.

With this in mind it is refreshing to come upon the work of Paul Bannick. The photographer/naturalist has not simply produced another book with exceptional photographs of birds; he has advanced the entire field of nature study by revealing the remarkable relationships that exist between woodpeckers and other species, particularly owls. Through Bannick's lenses and his thoughtful compositions, the larger world of nature comes into view as his subjects go about the business of home building, grooming, courtship, raising families, squabbling with competitors, or intently searching out their next meal. Such intimacy with nature produces profound empathy for these species and can only have been achieved by what the photographer refers to as his "inch by inch" movement into the lives of his subjects.

With patience, persistence, and a singular respect for his subject, Paul Bannick has produced a work that will endure. While it will certainly remain a constant reference to what is attractive and compelling in the behavior and appearance of birds, it will also continue to provide an example of how the fabric of nature is so carefully and intricately composed and what we might find there if we are willing to look long and deeply enough. These truthful and breathtaking images in company with informative narrative strengthen our footing for forays to the field where we can partake of the infinite wisdom that awaits us there.

—Tony Angell

Opposite: A female Northern Pygmy-Owl pops up from the depths of her cavity to trade calls with her mate outside.

Introduction

While teaching a snowshoeing navigation class one winter afternoon in Washington's Cascade Mountains, I decided to investigate a silver fir at the edge of a forest opening. Prying back a heavy and prickly branch, I stepped inside the skirt of the tree and saw a pair of bright yellow eyes staring at me from the catlike face of a small brown owl. My heart raced; I did not know what to do. I felt almost giddy to see a creature from my dreams, at eye level, his face less than three feet from my own. As I moved closer, the owl's eyes grew wider and his body lengthened. What species was he? Would he attack? Would he flush and be eaten by a raven or hawk? Why was he here? I thought I should leave him alone, but first I tried to commit to memory every distinctive feature—the triangular white eyebrows, the soft cream-colored streaks, the golden eyes, and the sharp talons—before carefully but awkwardly backing out on my snowshoes and opening a new chapter in my nature pursuits. I would never venture into the wilds again without my camera. I later learned that what I had seen was a Northern Saw-whet Owl.

This bird was the first new species of owl I had seen since I was a young boy. Back then, I had found the diversity of life in the fields, willow thickets, ponds, and streams near my suburban Pacific Northwest home fascinating. I was always finding a new bird, amphibian, or insect to identify, and discovering and learning about a species that was new to me provided my greatest joy and inspiration. While walking or running home after observing animals, I tried to remember their key markings and behaviors so that I could identify and read about them. When my efforts to memorize features proved unreliable, I tried drawing the critters and even went to the extreme of housing them in cages and aquariums, observing their behaviors while studying them in every book I could find.

At the same time I was saddened to see that much of the land on which I was finding these creatures was being bulldozed. I wondered if the development might be halted if people became aware of the wildlife living there. I showed my drawings to anyone who would pay attention, expressing my concerns about the destruction of the animals' habitats, but I felt that my hand-drawn pictures weren't compelling enough to motivate people to take action.

Photography seemed like a better option, so when I was twelve, I began using a camera instead of drawing to show people my favorite animals and places, hoping that someday my images might inspire protection of wild lands and wild creatures.

Birds were a big draw for me. While watching them in the field or at our backyard feeder, I wondered why I saw specific birds in certain seasons, where they came from, and what made their times of arrival so unpredictable. Flickers and Downy and Hairy Woodpeckers drew my undivided attention. I loved the flashes of red feathers, the maniacal calls, and the demonstrative drumming. On the other hand, owls were enigmas, with mystifying nocturnal lives and spiritlike calls. The first owl I ever saw, a Snowy Owl, appeared and disappeared quickly and without warning. To me, owls and woodpeckers were dramatic, mysterious, and distinctive, inspiring both deeply felt emotion and quiet contemplation. In short, they were nature's poetry.

While perusing my field guides, I would pause at pages of owls and woodpeckers and marvel at the variety of their colors, shapes, and sizes, daydreaming about what it would be like to find some of them. In my imagination, the colored areas on maps depicting their distributions had to be the wildest, most wonderful places. At the time, I could not imagine getting to those locales or actually seeing the birds. But the seeds had been planted.

As I grew older, I developed my photography and learned more about traveling in the wild. I took up backpacking, snowshoeing, sea kayaking, and navigation to get me to remote places where I could observe new animals. I learned to identify native plants and their habitats and compared topographic maps with distribution maps to locate specific plants and animals. Until five years ago, amphibians were my primary focus—I had observed only four species of woodpeckers and had had brief glimpses of

Opposite: A Yellow-shafted Northern Flicker returns to the nest cavity to feed his chicks.

only two owl species. That all changed when I encountered that Northern Saw-whet.

As often happens when I first discover a new animal, I began to research intensively—first owls and then woodpeckers—and I realized that I might indeed be able to find and photograph the birds I had marveled at in my youth. By studying the needs of

A Northern Saw-whet Owl freezes as he detects a shrew moving through the leaf litter below.

individual species and talking with knowledgeable folks, I learned to identify habitats, as well as the time of year, time of day, and locations where each might be found. In 2005 I upgraded my photo equipment and began a quest to photograph every species of owl and woodpecker in the West.

In my research, I noticed how the habitat requirements of birds often included the most unique and threatened components of their environments and I learned that many woodpeckers and owls are considered indicator species. An indicator species is dependent upon critical elements of a natural system and is the species most sensitive to degradation of those elements; the health of an indicator species population can be used to monitor the health of a natural system. Upon realizing this, I decided to photograph all the woodpeckers and owls of North America in hopes of drawing attention to the challenges facing these birds and their ecosystems. I explored the continent habitat by habitat, reaching out to local birding organizations, birders, and researchers, steeping myself in the subtleties of habitat requirements, life histories, distributions, and populations of birds to determine the best times and locations to visit.

In my travels, I photographed at the very first and very last light of day, when the light was best and most of the birds were most active. I sometimes stayed up all night, taking photos until the early hours of the morning. I reserved the middle of the day for evaluating sites, observing bird behavior and movements, reviewing images, and moving between locations.

I strove to capture a sense of intimacy with my subjects without disturbing them or changing their behavior. If a woodpecker or owl's behavior was altered, I changed my shooting location. Sometimes I spent hours moving inch by inch into the right position while I watched a bird's behaviors and movements, and the path of the sun. Once at my ideal location, I often waited hours for the right moment to unfold. Many of my photo trips did not yield any worthwhile images, but I always gained new knowledge about the birds, their habitats, or my photographic technique.

While studying owls and woodpeckers, I have been struck by the diversity within these two iconic groups of birds and the ways in which their presence both defines and enriches their habitats. The owl adds weight and spirit to wild places. It is an apical species, meaning it requires healthy populations of

A young Hairy Woodpecker calls for food from its cavity.

many species of plants and animals beneath it in its food web to survive. The woodpecker infuses bright colors and boisterous sounds into the landscape, while serving as a keystone bird in that, relative to its abundance, it exerts a disproportionately large influence on the structure and function of its ecosystem. These two bird groups are linked together by the fact that more than half of the owl species in North America rely in some part upon woodpeckers for their nest cavities.

Almost all the continent's terrestrial habitats host an owl, a woodpecker, or both, and in some complex landscapes several species of each can be found. It is understandable, then, why owls and woodpeckers have been studied and even revered in North America by many individuals and peoples, from Great Plains tribes to explorer Meriwether Lewis to the Inupiat of the Arctic. But these birds also serve a practical role in humans' lives. As natural pest-control agents, most owls feed on rodents, including rats and mice that might otherwise consume crops or invade homes. Woodpeckers and some owls consume prodigious quantities of insects, including such banes of homeowners as carpenter ants and termites, as well as adult and larval beetles and moths that wreak havoc on certain trees and forests.

My goal with the photographs and writing in this book is to increase awareness of these birds and their habitats, which in many cases are at risk. Although some species live in many parts of North America, the species highlighted in the pages that follow are presented within the broad habitat whose unique features they rely upon most. I hope the images and narrative presented in this book will inspire appreciation not only for the diversity of North America's owls and woodpeckers, but also for the extent to which they depend upon one another and the other animals and plants of each habitat.

After vigorously shaking her body, a Snowy Owl fluffs out her feathers before settling down to rest for the day.

Acknowledgments

Many people contributed to bringing this book to fruition, especially Shuna Klaveness, D.V.M., who generously and skillfully reviewed my manuscript throughout its iterations, providing invaluable input. I also appreciate the efforts of Katy Love, who graciously reviewed my writing, and offered insightful improvements.

My time in the field seeking and photographing owls and woodpeckers was my favorite part of the process. I had amazing experiences with fascinating subjects in inspiring places, and I met wonderful people along the way. Although I was usually alone when I photographed, I want to thank the many generous people who shared information and expertise that helped me locate birds in unfamiliar parts of the continent, especially Mike and MerryLynn Denny. Throughout the past few years, they have taught me a lot about specific species of owls, and that has served me well as I worked to photograph and write about them. Mike also contributed interesting facts after reviewing the manuscript.

Several people assisted me both in my expeditions and in reviewing photos, especially Wenyan Guo, who offered numerous hours of support, and Matt Bannick, William Bannick, Stephen Bannick, Melissa Chaun, Mark Christiansen, Claire Eldridge, Donna Perry, Dan Thrush, and Becky Uhler, who assisted me in the field.

I am grateful to several researchers, conservation professionals, and birders who shared their expertise and knowledge of specific species habitats and locations with me in the field or through their review and critique of relevant portions of my manuscript: Dennis Abbate, Jamie Acker, Christian Artuso, Brady Beck, Susan Campbell, Jannelle Cuddeford, Herb Curl, Bill Duyck, Elizabeth Evans, Cassidy Grattan, Karen Haire, Steve Hallstrom, Randy Hill, Denver Holt, David Hutchison, Lee Johnson, Brian Linkhart, Keith Kingdon, Mac Knight, Jeff Kozma, Kevin Mack, Genevieve Margherio, Alex Morgan, Tom Munson, Bob Person, Nathan Pieplow, Glenn Proudfoot, Keith Rankin, Richard Repp, John and Sue Rogers, Penny Rose, Mat Seidensticker, Curtis Smalling, Andy Stepniewski, John Stroud, Bob Sundstrom, George Vlahakis, Stewart Wechsler, Jack Whitman, Ron Wolf, and Scott Yanco. I would also like to thank the Arizona Game and Fish Department Research Branch and Endangered Species Branch of the Department of the Army–Fort Bragg Military Installation.

Thanks are due to those who introduced me to people who helped me with this endeavor including Keith Barnes, Ellen Blackstone, Nina Carter, John Gerwin, and Chris Peterson.

My thanks also go to Pam Kingdon, Lisa Whitman, and Margaret Bannick who welcomed me into their homes with warm hospitality, and Karen Hunke, who accommodated me at the El Tecolote Ranch.

I also wish to thank Tony Angell for offering valuable advice along the way and writing the foreword; Peter Jackson for being the first to encourage me to pursue my dream of publishing a book of my photography; and Paul Balle, Theresa Bannick, Kyle Bollmeier, Colby Chester, Mark Crickmore, Mark Gardiner, Mary Greenfield, Bryan Love, Klaus Richter, George and Kathy Smith, Diane Quinn, Barbara Van Heyningen, Ginny Schweigler, Ann Wahl, and especially Joe Bannick and Phil and Katy Vogelzang for their project-long support of my photographic efforts.

I am grateful to Mitch Friedman of Conservation Northwest for allowing me the flexibility in my work schedule that was necessary to complete this book.

I also would like to thank Martyn Stewart, who produced and contributed the CD of owl and woodpecker calls that accompanies this book.

Finally thanks go to Helen Cherullo for helping me make my book idea a reality, and to Linda Gunnarson, Heath Lynn Silberfeld, Mary Metz, Kate Rogers, and Mayumi Thompson for their hard work editing and designing the book.

OWL AND WOODPECKER HABITATS

- PACIFIC COAST URBAN & SUBURBAN
- NORTHWESTERN MARITIME FORESTS
- WESTERN DRY MOUNTAIN FORESTS
- WESTERN OAK WOODLANDS
- GRASSLANDS & SHRUB-STEPPE
- SOUTHWESTERN DRY LANDS
- SOUTHEASTERN PINE FORESTS
- EASTERN URBAN & SUBURBAN
- NORTHEASTERN FORESTS
- BOREAL FOREST
- ARCTIC TUNDRA
- OTHER

500 MILES

500 KM

1

Pacific Coast Urban and Suburban Habitats

Owls and woodpeckers are often regarded as inhabitants of North America's wildest places. While that is true of many, the open woodlands of suburban parks, gardens, and even backyards also provide habitat for some of the continent's most recognizable owl and woodpecker species. And in cities and suburbs along the Pacific Coast, several species native to more open areas in neighboring forests have adapted well to human presence.

While growing up in a Pacific Northwest suburb, I wasn't as interested in birds as in amphibians—until I saw a **Red-shafted Northern Flicker**. Accustomed to the browns and blacks of smaller birds at the feeder, I thought this woodpecker's red mustache was both humorous and dazzling, complementing the hint of red shafts on its folded wings. Its black-spotted breast, powerful chisel-shaped beak, and aggressive hopping gait amused and intrigued me. For the next several years I learned all I could about Flickers and other Northwest birds, and the Red-shafted Flicker became for me an iconic symbol for the woodland-edge habitat of the region—from greenbelts to pastures to rural, suburban, and even urban parks.

The Northern Flicker is North America's second-largest woodpecker after the Pileated Woodpecker. The combination of its large size and brown base color distinguish it from all other North American woodpeckers; the red mustache (found in males) and red underwings distinguish the Red-shafted subspecies from the Yellow-shafted, which is found in the East and Midwest.

Occurring in open woodland, woodland edge, and grassland habitat throughout most of the United States and Canada, the Northern Flicker is North America's most widely distributed woodpecker. The Red-shafted is found from coastal British Columbia to Mexico. It mingles with the Yellow-shafted subspecies in a narrow strip that extends from southeastern Alaska along the eastern edge of the Rocky Mountains to northern Texas, creating the occasional hybrid. The width of this zone is essentially the same as it was in the mid-1800s and marks the transition between two climates: the wetter eastern North America and the generally drier West. Many of the northern populations of Northern Flickers, including some of the hybrids, migrate south in winter; the hybrids often confuse bird-watchers trying to figure out which subspecies they have encountered.

The Red-shafted Flicker is for the most part a habitat generalist; its only requirements are open areas in which to forage and large dead trees, dead branches on large trees, or nest boxes in which to nest. It can acclimate easily to humans and will nest in small suburban backyards, yet it can also be found in some of the wildest parts of the western mountains.

Opposite: The male Red-shafted Northern Flicker is distinguished from the female by his red "malar," also frequently referred to as his "mustache."

Two competing female Red-shafted Northern Flickers display to one another.

Although not specialized in its habitat, the Red-shafted Flicker is specialized in its diet, preferring ants. Its brown base color hides it as it forages for ants on the ground. This Flicker also will eat beetle larvae and other insects and switches to fruit, berries, and suet when insects are unavailable. It has the longest tongue of any woodpecker, which it can extend more than 1.6 inches beyond the tip of its bill into an insect hole. It feels around with its tongue, spears its prey, and draws it into its bill.

As many suburban westerners can attest, Red-shafted Flickers can be loud, especially during the early part of breeding season in March, when frenzied rivals rap their sunrise drumming atop the most resonant objects in their territories, which are often metal chimneys or the sides of houses. Flickers have two common calls: a contact call, *wik-a-wik-a-wik-a*, and a long, steady song described as *kwikwikwikwi.*

Although Northern Flickers are still common, it is alarming that some populations have declined 30 percent over the last forty years. The scarcity of suitable dead wood for cavities appears to be the main reason for this decline. Competition from nonnative European starlings is another factor, as these aggressive birds will often evict a pair of Flickers just after they excavate a nest cavity.

Northern Flickers are prolific cavity excavators, usually creating at least one new cavity every year. They rarely reuse a cavity, although they often nest in one initiated the year before but completed in the current year. Cavities are excavated in a variety

Western Screech-Owls peer from a cavity in an old oak tree in a partially cryptic posture with their ear-tufts raised for camouflage.

of materials, although snags (dead trees) or dead portions of live trees are favored.

An interesting study conducted in the interior of British Columbia monitored twenty cavity-nesting birds and eight cavity-nesting mammals in a Douglas-fir ecosystem over an eight-year period. The study revealed that the Northern Flicker was the most abundant woodpecker, creating cavities large enough and numerous enough to support a majority of these species; the study labeled the Northern Flicker the keystone species in this ecosystem. Red-shafted Northern Flickers seem to play a similar role in all their habitats throughout western North America. In rural and suburban areas, a range of animals, including Douglas squirrels, flying squirrels, short-tailed weasels, American kestrels, black-capped chickadees, western bluebirds, tree swallows, buffleheads, Northern Saw-whet Owls, and Western Screech-Owls, nest in vacated Flicker cavities. In fact, of the more than eighty species of birds in North America that nest in cavities, roughly 25 percent can be found in the Pacific Northwest, and many of these nest only in woodpecker holes. In the Pacific Northwest, almost one-third of all forest vertebrate species nest or roost in cavities, and most are obligate cavity nesters, meaning they have no other choice. The vast majority of cavities are the work of woodpeckers.

Leaving older trees standing, imitating the woodland edge habitat in the gardens of parks and large yards, and installing nest boxes can aid in retaining healthy populations of this important architect of western habitats.

The availability of nest cavities, particularly those created by Northern Flickers, is a critical population constraint for the **Western Screech-Owl**, a small owl with golden eyes and prominent ear tufts. Nest cavities can be challenging for these owls to find in suburban locations, where snags and dead branches—woodpeckers' favorites for drilling—are often removed for cleanup or safety reasons. Where suitable Northern Flicker, Gilded Flicker, or Pileated Woodpecker cavities are not available, Western Screech-Owls will use natural cavities or nest boxes. Fights over cavities are common, and these owls are known to evict Northern Flickers. Unlike many owls, they sometimes use the same cavity several years in a row.

The Western Screech-Owl occurs in a variety of habitats from southeast Alaska to Mexico, attaining its highest density in low-lying deciduous woodlands close to water and other riparian areas. These are often the same areas that are developed for human habitation, which has resulted in declining Western Screech-Owl populations. Fortunately, this owl tolerates people and often nests in residential neighborhoods and city parks when large old trees with cavities are present. It particularly favors bigleaf maple in the Northwest, oaks in California, cottonwoods in drier areas,

A Hairy Woodpecker excavates a cavity in a quaking aspen tree.

saguaro cacti in the Southwest, and large fruit trees throughout its range. When these conditions are met, populations can be quite dense, as Western Screech-Owls probably benefit from a lack of natural predators along with the availability of their own prey, such as house sparrows and mice, whose populations are always high in residential areas.

Western Screech-Owls are not migratory, and their movements are limited to the young dispersing after fledging. At that time, linked habitat in the form of greenbelts, yards with mature trees, and parks makes it possible for the young owls to find new territories and older individuals to recruit new mates.

During winter, Western Screech-Owls roost in conifers, but as trees leaf out in spring, they are effectively camouflaged on deciduous roosts, particularly when in their cryptic (camouflaged) posture with eyes closed and ear tufts raised. They can also be quite inconspicuous while hunting. I have seen these owls motionless, balancing at the end of a bigleaf maple twig and casting only a leaf-size silhouette against the moonlit sky while waiting for prey to appear.

Western Screech-Owls are nocturnal and hunt by pouncing on prey that moves underneath their perches. They eat almost all living fauna small enough to subdue, including rodents, insects, birds, fish, crayfish, worms, and frogs. In Seattle, these owls seem to have a taste for earthworms and are hilarious to watch as they suck them down like long noodles.

These owls are particularly aggressive hunters when feeding their young. I was reviewing images on my laptop alongside an enclosed courtyard one May afternoon in Tucson. The sun was scorching, so I was under the eave of a building. Out of the corner of my eye, I saw a dark shape drop suddenly from the roof to the ground. "Owl," I thought, and crept into the courtyard to verify my hunch. A Western Screech-Owl sat on the ground in the midday sun with a mourning dove in its talons. Presumably this owl was breaking the nocturnal hunting rule in order to satisfy his young.

Western Screech-Owls are often mobbed by mixed flocks of songbirds, which dive at them, attacking with beak or claws and calling loudly. This generates little reaction, but should a crow, jay, or raven make itself known, nesting pairs will drive it away, as these are potential nest predators. They also will react aggressively to the calls of Northern Spotted Owls and Great Horned Owls, to whom they can fall prey. Barred Owls also may hunt them, and some concern has been expressed in the Pacific Northwest, where

Pausing between calls for food, a fledgling Western Screech-Owl waits to be fed.

populations are noticeably reduced, that Barred Owls are responsible. The only places I still find Screech-Owls near my home are ravines with mature bigleaf maples.

Plumage color varies across the Western Screech-Owl's range, often matching the bark of its nesting or roosting tree. During one memorable encounter, my companion grinned and pointed at an oak snag no more than thirty feet from us, saying, "The owl is in that old tree." I pride myself on being able to spot well-camouflaged birds from moving vehicles and while paddling kayaks on Puget Sound, so I felt sure I would be able to detect this bird without difficulty. But I strained to see a golden eye or mismatched feather. Finally I saw it: it looked exactly like a weathered, light-gray fragment of wood with two matching spikes (its ear tufts) partially eclipsing the opening of a large cavity in the weathered gray tree.

The demands of feeding young occasionally motivate Western Screech-Owls to capture prey, such as this dove, in broad daylight.

Size also varies, and nine Western Screech-Owl subspecies have been named based upon size and color. Those from the Pacific Northwest are mostly brown or gray brown, with a small percentage of reddish brown coastal specimens. Owls from drier areas east of the Cascades and in California and Arizona vary from dark to pale gray in desert terrain. Populations with the same base color have variable black markings. For example, gray individuals I photographed near Tucson, Arizona, looked markedly different from those near Sierra Vista, just ninety miles away.

Sizes increase from south to north and from lowland to inland mountains, with the largest individuals inhabiting the Pacific Northwest interior. The feet are feathered in the north-

ern populations and bristled in deserts in the south. Females in all populations are slightly larger than males.

Screech-Owl species are most easily differentiated by sound, as physical differences between Western, Eastern, and Whiskered Screech-Owls are subtle. The Western Screech-Owl has several different calls, but the most distinctive and distinguishing is the "bouncing ball" call that is best described as a series of whistled *hoots* that become more tightly spaced toward their conclusion. Calling begins early in the breeding season (late winter or early spring) and lasts until the end of spring. These birds are then generally quiet until the young disperse, usually by September.

Physical differences between the three Screech-Owl species include the Western Screech-Owl's black (gray in the

Opposite: Spying a new food source, a Downy Woodpecker prepares to fly.

Pacific Northwest) bill color compared to the yellowish to light-green bill of the Eastern Screech-Owl. The Whiskered Screech-Owl is 25 percent smaller than the other two, with a yellowish-olive bill and a faint brownish neck ring. It is found

A male Hairy Woodpecker waits for a mate to join him at his freshly excavated cavity in a red alder.

living near Western Screech-Owls only in the mountains of far southeastern Arizona.

Like the Western Screech-Owl, **Downy Woodpeckers** and **Hairy Woodpeckers** show gradient differences in color. Those on the East Coast show much more white down their backs, and as one moves west they become darker. It is interesting that in areas of higher humidity, such as the coastal Pacific Northwest, they have darker, sootier breasts.

Downy and Hairy Woodpeckers are often mistaken for each other, as both are predominantly black woodpeckers with white spots, a white stripe down the back, and red on the back of the male's head. The Hairy is a medium-size woodpecker with a bill longer than its head. In contrast, the Downy is the smallest woodpecker in North America with a bill that is shorter than its head.

Drumming is for woodpeckers what songs are for perching songbirds. Both Downy and Hairy Woodpeckers do more than their share, drumming throughout the year to establish territory, attract a mate, and communicate location. The most common vocalization for both birds is the monosyllabic *peek* call, which is louder and lower pitched in the Hairy.

Although the Downy and Hairy look and sound similar, their behavior and habitat show marked differences. With its smaller size and smaller bill, the Downy Woodpecker is an opportunistic Lilliputian, climbing slender stalks of weeds and hanging upside down from brittle twigs or berries in pursuit of insects. Its bill is weaker and less chisel shaped than the Hairy's and is used differently, often like a pick to pursue insects on a branch surface or just below the surface. At other times, it uses its bill like tweezers to dig out individual insect eggs. In excavating a nest cavity, it chooses soft snags and branches in advanced stages of decay.

The Hairy Woodpecker uses its strong chisel-shaped bill to scrape up insects, particularly ants in large conifers. It also feeds on beetle larvae in burns, as well as on adult beetles and larvae during bark beetle outbreaks. Throughout North America this woodpecker has helped control populations of such problem insects as codling moths and elm bark beetles (responsible for the devastating Dutch elm disease).

Downy and Hairy Woodpeckers are nonmigratory, although both wander in winter, when they may be seen in urban and suburban yards and parks. The Downy reaches its greatest density among deciduous trees with low canopies, which often can be found in backyards and orchards. In these places, the Downy seems fairly tame and allows close approach, particularly on cold winter days. The Hairy is much less confiding and is found only among conifers paired with a significant understory of deciduous shrubs or small trees.

Although the Hairy Woodpecker can be found in lowland coniferous woodlands, it is most abundant in mid-elevation mixed-coniferous forests, where the cavities it creates are utilized by a variety of animals, including bluebirds and Flammulated Owls, and serve as the cavity of choice for the Northern Pygmy-Owl. Hairy Woodpeckers create most of the medium-size cavities found in coniferous and mixed coniferous forests. They usually prefer to excavate from scratch in live trees with fungal rot, but occasionally they enlarge cavities initially hammered out by Downy Woodpeckers. Once created, these valuable cavities must be defended if flying squirrels try to usurp them or Screech-Owls, house sparrows, Red-bellied Woodpeckers, or European starlings threaten to take the woodpeckers' young.

Throughout the cities and suburbs of the Pacific Coast, from Vancouver, British Columbia, to San Diego, California, a surprising amount of habitat for owls and woodpeckers exists in parks, greenbelts, and backyards. The primary threat to all woodpeckers and owls in these suburban and urban areas is the removal of dead branches and snags in the process of tidying up for safety or aesthetic reasons. This all-too-common practice dooms populations of cavity-nesting birds, and it has contributed to the decline in Northern Flicker numbers throughout North America. When Flicker numbers decline, numbers of a whole host of other animals, such as Western Screech-Owls, western bluebirds, and Northern Saw-whet Owls, also decline.

Since urban and suburban areas are fragments of surrounding habitat, replicating outlying natural areas in parks and backyards presents the best chance of preserving and enhancing habitat for owls and woodpeckers. Planting native plants and removing invasive ones improves habitat and preserves biodiversity, and it also aids in the dispersal of young birds and recruitment of mates by linking habitats. In areas where surface streams have been channeled into subterranean pipes, removing the pipes and bringing the running water back to the surface, as well as creating ponds and other water features, can create riparian habitat and mimic wetlands that provide fresh water for drinking, bathing, and attracting prey. In places that lack trees large enough

Incapable of creating their own cavities, western bluebirds often nest in those created by woodpeckers.

to accommodate cavities, nest boxes can be provided for cavity nesters, such as Red-shafted Flickers and Western Screech-Owls. In addition, since pesticides and herbicides reduce food supplies and are potentially toxic to birds, reducing or limiting their use and planting berries and fruit-bearing plants that are attractive to birds could sustain a healthier environment for all species, including humans.

2

Northwestern Maritime Forests

The Northwestern maritime forests stretch along the Pacific Coast from the coastal redwoods of northern California and north throughout much of the mixed cedar, hemlock, and spruce conifer forests west of the Cascade Crest to southeast Alaska (excluding Washington's Puget Sound region, a relatively dry area receiving only 30 to 40 inches of rain a year in which "rainy" Seattle lies, and Oregon's Willamette Valley). These lush forests receive more than 60 inches of rainfall annually, with some receiving as much as 180 inches. As for all forests, fire has played a historic role in their succession. These forests are hit by infrequent stand-replacing fires, in which all the trees in the affected area are killed, as compared to the frequent low-intensity burns that historically shaped dry forests by thinning the understory but rarely killed the dominant older trees.

Old-growth stands in these Pacific Northwest forests are characterized by closed canopies supported by giant trees up to 260 feet tall and 10 feet in diameter. Although the canopy is closed, the variety of tree sizes still allows light to hit the cone-laden forest floor, promoting the growth of an abundance of perennial plants, shrubs, and shade-tolerant trees, such as western hemlock and Pacific silver fir. Although the less shade-tolerant Douglas-firs cannot compete under a canopy, they grow fastest when the forests are young and they are the giants soaring above the canopy in scattered locales where red tree voles (prey for the Northern Spotted Owl) feed upon their needles. Clearings formed by fires, floods, wind, and landslides create forest openings for new Douglas-fir saplings, as well as Sitka spruce and western red cedar in wetter areas. Immense vertical snags with fist-size holes carved by Pileated Woodpeckers serve as nest sites for northern flying squirrels, and in every direction colossal rotting logs nurse sapling conifers.

A friend and I drove into the rainy coastal forests of Lane County, Oregon, and entered the territory of a pair of **Northern Spotted Owls**. From the dirt road, the forest was a wall of many different greens. Pulling back a low bough of a giant western red cedar was like opening a door to a cool room. Beyond this limb, a green carpet plunged more than sixty degrees, but the old moss-laden logs that littered the hillside made it impossible to see how far it fell before reaching a stream below. Similarly, when I looked up I could see neither sky nor the highest ceiling of the forest. Beyond each fanlike layer of green was another, until they blended into pale green light. The forest was dark, but shafts of filtered light illuminated sword ferns, Oregon grape, salmonberry, and the glossy green cattail moss blanketing every surface.

We expected to descend into the ravine before calling an

Opposite: A Northern Spotted Owl follows prey with his eyes before swooping down to seize it.

owl in, but the owl found us. As soon as we paused, she flew in and landed a few feet above our heads, watching us intently with her round, dark eyes. This was typical of my encounters with these owls. To photograph most birds and mammals, I use stealth to approach them slowly and stand motionless as they gaze at me or flee, but every time I have found a Northern Spotted Owl, it was already looking at me. Even when I have looked for them in reliable places and failed to find them, I have sensed that they were watching me and that I simply failed to see them as they watched.

The Northern Spotted Owl was listed as "threatened" under the Endangered Species Act in 1990 and it has few predators, but it is now in grave danger of extinction. Fewer than 3,000 pairs and 1,000 unpaired individuals remain in North America, with populations in British Columbia and Washington particularly hard hit. As of 2007, only an estimated 23 Northern Spotted Owls were left in British Columbia, while Washington had roughly 300 to 550 pairs remaining. Overall, the population is declining by about 6 percent a year. Between 2000 and 2007, the population of Northern Spotted Owls in Washington State fell by approximately 50 percent.

Given its critical situation and the surrounding controversy, this dark brown bird with small, white, irregular spots on much of its body is one of the most studied owls in the world.

Northern Spotted Owls require old-growth forests such as this maritime forest along the Oregon coast.

Weak excavators such as the red-breasted nuthatch benefit from the presence of Pileated Woodpeckers because the woodpeckers' drilling speeds the decomposition of trees.

It lacks ear tufts and has a large round face with a distinctive brown facial disk, dark brown eyes, and completely feathered legs and feet. Females are larger than males but otherwise the sexes look alike. It is likely to be confused only with the Barred Owl, but the Barred is slightly larger, has horizontal bars rather than spots on the breast, has vertical streaks on the abdomen, and appears grayer overall.

The Northern Spotted Owl is one of three subspecies of Spotted Owl, along with the Mexican Spotted Owl and the California Spotted Owl. All are very similar in appearance, although the plumage on the Northern Spotted Owl is darker and the spots are smaller. The primary call is a low-pitched series of *hoots* referred to as the "four-note location call," which consists of a single *hoot* with a short pause, two tightly placed *hoots*, and a final fading *hoot*. The Northern Spotted Owl is nonmigratory, but the other two subspecies show some altitudinal movement within territories throughout the year.

The Northern Spotted inhabits closed-canopy old-growth forests from southern British Columbia to northern California and ranges from moist coastal forests to nearby subalpine areas. Older forests are required, as large trees with trunks over three feet thick are a critical habitat element. These forests provide the complex understory and multistoried canopies that serve this species' hunting, roosting, and nesting requirements.

This bird's affinity for the multiple canopies afforded by ancient forests results from their intolerance of heat stress. Northern Spotted Owls typically roost in densely vegetated areas with the densest cover above their heads, presumably as protection against weather and predators such as goshawks and Great Horned Owls. During cold weather they often roost high in the

Next page: Northern Spotted Owls hunt within the forest canopy, moving from limb to limb, listening and looking for food.

canopy to take advantage of rising warmer air; during warmer summer days they descend to lower, cooler spots, particularly in proximity to streams.

The Northern Spotted Owl's food choices demonstrate a preference for hunting well above the ground within the old-growth forest canopy, rather than pouncing upon terrestrial prey. It feeds mostly on small mammals that move among the limbs of trees, especially flying squirrels in the northern part of its range, with wood rats becoming an increasing part of its diet south of the Oregon Cascades. Food availability determines the size of its home range, with larger home ranges existing where flying squirrels are the primary food item. Other prey include red tree voles and other small mammals, birds (including the Northern Pygmy-Owl and Western Screech-Owl), amphibians, and even bats, which they sometimes hunt on the wing.

Primarily a nocturnal hunter, the Northern Spotted Owl usually perches and waits for prey to approach, then silently glides in to make a kill. Peak hunting occurs just after sunset and just before sunrise, but roosting birds will sometimes seize the opportunity to take prey moving below them. Although agile on the wing while hunting, the Spotted Owl usually flies indirectly within the canopy, moving from perch to perch as it ascends or descends rather than making one direct flight. It typically avoids crossing over or hunting in open or brushy areas, including clear-cuts, recently logged areas, or burns, although it occasionally hunts at the forest edge.

Ancient trees, primarily live ones, provide the nesting platforms needed by this species. Chimneys and cavities created by the broken tops and branches of trees supply the majority of nest sites, but sometimes the abandoned nests of goshawks and ravens or dense mats of dwarf mistletoe or accumulated forest debris are used. Pairs sometimes reuse the nest from the previous year, and pairings are long lasting. Unlike some owls, Northern Spotteds are not very territorial and often have overlapping territories. Sometimes unmated males will live within the territory of a mated pair until the opportunity to mate presents itself. That said, Northern Spotted Owls require a territory of up to three-quarters of a square mile to meet food and nesting requirements.

Northern Spotted Owl populations are challenged by low

The Northern Spotted Owl moves within the canopy of old-growth coast forests in response to changes in temperature.

reproductive success. Not all pairs breed every year, and although one to four eggs might be laid by those that do breed, most successful pairs fledge only one or two owlets per nesting attempt. Once fledged, less than one-third of juveniles survive to adulthood. Fortunately, Northern Spotted Owl adults have a much higher annual survival rate (as high as 90 percent) than other owl species and can live more than fifteen years in the wild.

The continued loss of old-growth forests to timber harvest, as well as lag effects from past loss, are still the biggest

Opposite: Red-breasted Sapsuckers serve as a keystone species in maritime forests both for the cavities they create and the sap wells, relied upon by rufous hummingbirds and others, they drill.

One young Northern Spotted Owl watches as his sibling attempts to remove the downy fledgling feathers.

factors in this bird's decline. The lack of proper habitat impacts prey, thermoregulation, and reproduction and creates greater exposure to common predators such as the goshawk and Great Horned Owl. Old-growth harvest isolates Northern Spotted Owl territories, making the post-breeding dispersal of young and the replacement of lost mates even more difficult. The harvest of habitat still occurs; more than 50,000 acres of Northern Spotted Owl habitat on state and private lands were logged in the past decade alone, the majority of which were in western Washington.

The range expansion of the Barred Owl, the Spotted Owl's close relative, has added more pressure to dwindling populations. This slightly larger, stronger, and more aggressive owl arrived in the Pacific Northwest in the 1970s, but over the last decade populations have exploded. Unfortunately, evidence suggests that the more adaptive Barred Owl has been displacing the Northern Spotted Owl in many areas, breeding with it in others, and perhaps even preying upon it.

The Barred Owl's presence may be harming the Northern Spotted Owl in indirect ways, too. Over the last few years, researchers have noticed that Northern Spotted Owls stop calling or responding to calls when Barred Owls are in the vicinity. When Barred Owls are removed, Northern Spotted Owls resume their calling. This behavior has critical implications, as surveying and monitoring to determine an owl's presence rely upon three years of surveying to determine occupation. If a site is considered unoccupied by these owls, timber harvest is sometimes approved, though this is becoming less common.

The Northern Spotted Owl is an indicator species for Pacific Northwest old-growth forest; in other words, the state of this bird represents the state of these forests. In this role, it has become an icon of efforts to preserve old-growth forests in the region. The northwestern maritime forests contain the fastest-growing and some of the most commercially valuable timber in North America. High demand for this timber has made it challenging to protect the remaining old-growth forest. If this old-growth forest is lost, an entire ecosystem that is represented by, but not limited to, the Northern Spotted Owl will be lost.

As they do in every forested habitat in North America, woodpeckers serve keystone roles in the moist forests of the Pacific Northwest. Red-breasted Sapsuckers, which prefer old-growth habitat, tap sugar-rich sap for rufous hummingbirds before flower nectar is available. Pileated Woodpeckers aid in the forest decomposition process by breaking down trees into smaller, more easily decomposed pieces and creating dozens of huge nesting, roosting, and feeding cavities each year that serve the needs of several animals too large to use cavities created by smaller woodpeckers. Among the tenants of Pileated Woodpecker cavities are the Northern Spotted Owl's preferred prey, the northern flying squirrel, and several old-growth-dependent "species of concern," such as the fisher, American marten, silver-haired bat, and common merganser, as well as Vaux's swift, which is on the "sensitive species" lists of both Washington and Oregon.

The Northern Spotted Owl faces extinction if current trends continue, but if we strengthen Endangered Species Act protections, conserve remaining old-growth northwestern forests, and continue vigilant study of nesting and habitat fragmentation while aggressively responding to threats, we will improve the odds that our grandchildren can be "discovered" by this mystical owl or stopped in their tracks by its stirring call as they explore the forests of the Pacific Northwest.

3

Western Dry Mountain Forests

The dry mountain forests of the West range from east of the Cascade Crest south through the Sierra Nevada and east through much of the Rocky Mountains. They also include parts of ranges in between, including the Okanogan Highlands, the Kettle River Range, the eastern Blue Mountains, and isolated ranges across the central and northern Great Basin.

Historically, these forests were shaped by periodic low-intensity fires, which removed smaller trees and shrubs but left older ponderosa pine and the drought-resistant variety of Douglas-fir, both of which have thick, fire-resistant bark. The forests host the most diverse assemblage of conifers and the greatest diversity of owls and woodpeckers in North America. Eleven of the nineteen owls and thirteen of the twenty-two woodpeckers of North America breed in this habitat.

Habitat changes gradually from north to south and also changes with elevation. The "life zone" concept developed by C. Hart Merriam is a way to describe places with similar plant and animal communities and explains the diversity found in mountainous areas like the western dry mountains. Merriam noticed that, all things being equal, a 1,000-foot gain in elevation was equivalent to traveling 300 miles north. This concept helps explain both the ecological diversity found on North America's steep terrain and how mountains at different latitudes in the

Cascades, Rockies, and Sierra Nevada might provide similar habitats for specific birds while adjacent lowlands are home to very different species. Illustrating this concept, since the North Cascades in Okanogan County, Washington, are approximately 600 miles north of Yuba Pass in the northern Sierra, it's not surprising that habitats near Yuba Pass at 6,000 feet are similar to those found in the North Cascades at 4,000 feet.

Throughout the western dry mountain forests, even east of the mountain crests, the subalpine areas often reflect the maritime forests, both in the amount of rain that falls upon the Engelmann spruce, mountain hemlock, whitebark pine, and subalpine fir and because fires hit this region less frequently, and when they do, they tend to be dramatic, stand-replacing fires. Descending from this particular zone, the climate becomes increasingly warmer and drier.

The mixed conifer and conifer-deciduous areas found at middle elevations below the subalpine zone and above the ponderosa pine zone show signs of a fire-regulated ecosystem with the characteristic open understory. The composition and structure of these forests varies. In the dry forest zone of Washington's eastern Cascades, one typical mix often includes grand fir, ponderosa pine, Douglas-fir, lodgepole pine, western larch, and in some cases western white pine. In the Sierra, red fir

Opposite: A hungry Pileated Woodpecker chick anticipates the arrival of a parent with food.

While incubating her eggs, the female Northern Pygmy-Owl will periodically call for the male to bring food.

This particular mix of ponderosa pine, Douglas-fir, and quaking aspen in the Washington Cascades provides a rich habitat where Downy Woodpeckers, Hairy Woodpeckers, Red-shafted Northern Flickers, Northern Pygmy-Owls, Pileated Woodpeckers, Red-breasted Sapsuckers, Red-naped Sapsuckers, White-headed Woodpeckers, and Williamson's Sapsuckers all breed.

and various pines, cedars, and broadleaf evergreens are found. Quaking aspen grow wherever a disturbance like fire creates an opening, particularly where the soil is moist, such as near ponds, lakes, and streams.

Farther downslope, ponderosa pine and drought-resistant Douglas-fir become the dominant conifers. Douglas-fir predominates at higher elevations, on north-facing slopes, and in shadier locations as it can better withstand the colder temperatures, higher moisture, and weaker light. The taproot of the ponderosa pine allows it to thrive in hot, dry, south-facing

slopes and lower elevations. Many areas feature mixes of both, as ponderosa pine is better able to germinate in open areas and Douglas-fir can germinate in the light shade underneath the ponderosa pine and quickly equal its height. At the lowest elevations of most of this region, open parklike stands of only ponderosa pine feature herbaceous understories of the bordering grasslands and oak woodlands. At higher elevations of the eastern edge of the southern Sierra, Jeffrey pine, which can withstand colder temperatures and less water than ponderosa pine, takes its place. Cottonwoods grow primarily along streams in open areas at lower elevations, often mixed with stands of ponderosa pine, oak woodlands, and grasslands.

Violet grass widows and golden glacier lilies poked through patches of snow, Western larches were yet to bud, and the steady rolling drumming of Williamson's Sapsuckers echoed around me in the icy March dawn at 3,600 feet in a middle-elevation mixed-conifer forest on the east side of Washington's Cascade Mountains. A *toot* froze me. I knew a **Northern Pygmy-Owl** was close. My reply *toot* initiated a duet. We traded whistles while I frantically searched for the small, fierce bird, hoping to fix my

Burned trees with patches of bark removed are a signature of Black-backed Woodpeckers.

lens on him before he tired of our exchange. Pushing through swampy puddles and stumbling over foot-thick downed aspens, I nearly fell headlong into him, jerking back inches before contact. Glaring at me, his intense golden eyes fourteen inches from my own, he was unimpressed. I respectfully backed up and gave myself some focusing distance.

A few minutes later, the tooting resumed and confused me. I found myself circling the aspen grove and following the calls. I figured the owl must be flying from one end of the grove to the other. Finally I found him perched on a dead branch, calling intently. Fixing my lens on him, I was surprised to hear a loud trill as another owl quickly popped into the frame. Before I could move back to accommodate two owls, the male jumped on the female's back and they began to mate, with both chattering. Following mating, he perched beside her and they preened each other until she flew off.

Soon he was calling excitedly, drawing her again to his side. As she landed he departed, whipped by me, and flew into an abandoned Hairy Woodpecker cavity, then called again. As soon as the female responded, he departed. By following him with my lens, I missed capturing a photo of her as she flew into the cavity. They later nested in that cavity.

More than any wild animal I have observed, the Northern Pygmy-Owls were indifferent to my presence, allowing me to watch a wide range of behavior over several days. They never fled, never struck a defensive or cryptic posture, and sometimes perched less than seven feet off the ground.

The Northern Pygmy-Owl is tiny and plump with a small head, long tail, and short wings. The male is slightly smaller than the female. The base color is usually gray-brown, brown, or sometimes rufous (reddish), with color varying geographically. The grayest are found in the Rocky Mountains, the brownest on the Pacific Coast, and the most rufous in the southern part of the range.

White spots accent the plumage of this owl's forehead, and two "false eyes" are formed by plumage on the back of the head, presumably fooling predators and increasing chances of survival. The dark tail is crossed by several white bars and is normally held straight down or at a slight angle, although it can twitch up and down or side to side when the owl is excited or agitated. The toes are feathered.

It breeds throughout much of the western mountains in

After mating, two Northern Pygmy-Owls preen one another.

deciduous, coniferous, and mixed forests from southeast Alaska through western British Columbia, the Pacific Northwest, the western mountain states, and into parts of Latin America. Throughout its territory, this owl is found along the edges of the forest, where its preferred prey is most abundant and most easily located.

During the breeding season, these owls and their cavities are rarely found, both because they are so small and well camouflaged in their forested habitat and because, unlike some owls, Northern Pygmy-Owls will not come out of their nest cavity if their tree is tapped or scratched. They are easier to find during winter, when many venture into the lowlands in search of food, and they are often seen at the round terminus at the top of a tree or near bird-feeding areas while they are hunting.

Infamous as a fierce predator of birds, the Northern Pygmy-Owl also preys upon mammals and insects, particularly during breeding season. It hunts during the day, with the hunt peaking in the early and late hours. Its diet includes several species of lizards, small rodents, and birds. Several accounts of this ambitious owl tell of it taking on larger birds, including a California quail more than twice its size. It also forays into nest cavities of woodpeckers, preying on the young. The lack of such features as a well-defined facial disk, offset ears, or flight-silencing characteristics on the wing feathers hint that this bird hunts with its eyes.

The primary song of the Northern Pygmy-Owl, exercised throughout the year, is a single hollow *toot* with a pause of a second or two followed by another *toot*. The *toot* call differs in timing and repetition within its range, leading some to suggest that it should be divided into three subspecies.

Next page: After feeding her young, a Pileated Woodpecker flies from her nest cavity.

Pileated Woodpecker chicks aggressively compete for food.

descent to lowlands, this is not a migrating bird, and its movements are limited to flying from one forest patch to a neighboring one. Retaining connected habitats is important to allow juveniles to disperse and maintain genetically mixed populations.

An obligate cavity nester, the Northern Pygmy-Owl prefers holes created by the Hairy Woodpecker but will also nest in natural cavities and those created by other woodpeckers. Within its landscape, snags within conifer stands are important habitat elements.

The mixed coniferous forests of western mountains are home to a variety of other vertebrates that require cavities larger than those provided by the Hairy Woodpecker or even the Northern Flicker. Fortunately, the Cascades, Sierra Nevada, and Coast Ranges are home to the largest woodpecker in North America, the **Pileated Woodpecker**, which creates cavities twice the size of those provided by the Northern Flicker.

In the Pacific Northwest alone, more than twenty species of secondary cavity nesters use Pileated Woodpecker cavities. Large cavity nesters such as the wood duck, common goldeneye, bufflehead, hooded merganser, and Northern Hawk Owl, as well as the Pacific fisher and American marten, are too large to use cavities created by any other woodpecker.

On a camping trip in eastern Washington, the resounding greeting call of Pileated Woodpeckers—*whichew, whichew, whichew*—was my wake-up call, signaling that the sun had risen and the first Pileated Woodpecker was making contact with its mate, with feeding imminent. Hastily, I threw on my clothes, zipped open my tent, attached my camera to its tripod, flung the rig over my shoulder, and sprinted to my vantage point behind some downed aspens. For the next four hours I watched while parents brought wood-boring beetle larvae and carpenter ants to their pleading young.

Three crested young lunged their bony black-and-white necks out of the nest cavity, begging to be fed, one chick always louder and willing to bite its siblings to retain the right to be on top and get fed first. After the mother had emptied her mouth and throat completely into the bills of the chicks, the more aggressive chick continued to thrust toward her, clamping onto her neck with its bill in hopes of gaining more.

The Pileated Woodpecker is referred to as "crow size," but

Although not common anywhere, Northern Pygmy-Owl populations do not appear to be in decline. Since this owl hunts at the edges of forests, clearings formed by burns and thinning of overgrown forests might improve its habitat. Except for its winter

Opposite: A male White-headed Woodpecker removes wood chips from his excavation in a ponderosa pine snag.

to me it seems a bit larger and certainly more striking. The adjective *pileated* means "crested," and both sexes sport a brilliant red crest, although on the larger male the red extends forward to the bill. A red malar or mustache also adorns the male, forming a narrow stripe that runs back from the base of the bill, merging into a black stripe that both sexes have on the sides of their necks. The large, chisel-like bill of this woodpecker enables it to craft impressive excavations.

Pileated Woodpeckers mate for life, and if a partner dies the surviving bird will defend its territory alone and try to recruit a new mate from a neighboring territory. New vertical oval-shaped nest cavities are excavated every year, with several partial cavities often created before a commitment is made to the final one. Cavities are defended, but these birds allow other cavity-nesting birds to nest in the same tree.

Once the young fledge, the adults dig additional cavities in which the young woodpeckers explore and roost. Each adult bird creates several roost cavities to use at night and during

Small secondary cavity nesters like this mountain chickadee benefit from abandoned nests of smaller primary excavators such as the Downy Woodpecker and Red-naped and Williamson's Sapsuckers.

bad weather. These cavities are often created in hollow trees or snags so that only the entrances require excavation. Usually Pileateds create several entrances to provide escape routes in case a predator enters.

These birds also excavate large feeding cavities as a by-product of their pursuit of wood-boring insects and insect larvae, frequently close to the ground. All these cavities and excavations tend to be chiseled as rectangular, horizontal shafts straight into stumps and snags. They require large, old trees and leave behind potential nests and habitat improvements for dozens of species. Although they often excavate in decayed wood, they are the only western woodpeckers that also excavate in heartwood, the denser core of the tree. They are probably responsible for infecting a significant percentage of trees throughout their range with heart rot, a disease that weakens the heartwood, thereby creating a suitable base for weaker excavators such as sapsuckers.

The Pileated will go to extreme lengths to pursue carpenter ants, ripping apart trees, excavating in snags until they topple, and prying off large sections of bark to gain access to the honeycombed nests. Other insect-eating birds, including other woodpeckers, take advantage of these excavations. The Pileated also eats wood-boring beetle larvae, fruit, berries, and even suet from feeders.

Although this bird emits several vocalizations, its territorial call is its most famous. It sounds a bit like a Northern Flicker but much louder and wilder and is used as the background call in jungle scenes of many old movies. This call is phoneticized as *cuk, cuk, cuk.* Its drumming is loud and slow like a drumroll that speeds up and becomes softer toward the finish.

The most dense populations of Pileated Woodpeckers are established in old-growth forests with an abundance of large, old trees in various states of decay. If such trees remain in other habitats, such as younger woodlands or even large parks, Pileateds can nest in them as well. These woodpeckers can be found in forested lands in much of the western and eastern United States and southern Canada.

Timber harvest can greatly reduce populations. Pileated Woodpeckers were nearly depleted in the eastern United States in the early 1900s after the land was cleared, but they rebounded after forests grew back. Populations throughout much of their range are stable now, but conversion of old-growth forests to

Two "false eyes" on the back of the Northern Pygmy-Owl's head are believed to discourage would-be predators from attacking at vulnerable times such as when the owl is feeding its young.

younger or single-age stands, removal of large nest snags, and fragmentation of habitat are all threats.

The U.S. Forest Service has identified the Pileated Woodpecker as a management indicator species of mature forest habitats and protects 120 hectares in old-growth forests for nesting and an additional 120 hectares with greater than five snags per hectare for foraging in Oregon and Washington. Despite these efforts, Pileated Woodpeckers are currently

Sapsuckers, like this male Red-naped, consume the sap their wells generate as well as the insects drawn to the sap.

candidates for endangered species listing by the Washington Department of Fish and Wildlife and are considered a "Species-at-Risk." Population declines of Pileateds could precipitate the decline of many species of wildlife that depend upon their excavations for shelter and food.

Western mountain slopes are dominated by conifers, but where the soil stays moist during the dry summer months, various deciduous trees thrive. In the northwest maritime forests, cavity nesters use red alder, bigleaf maple, black cottonwood, and bitter cherry, while on the drier eastern slopes cottonwood and quaking aspen, which grow in riparian areas, are the most important trees for cavity nesters. Most woodpeckers nest in the snags of these trees or in live trees infected with heart rot.

Quaking aspen is the most widespread tree in North America and is by far the most important for cavity-nesting birds, with dozens of species basing the limits of their territories upon it. This tree has thin living bark, and wounds caused by fire or woodpecker drillings can easily introduce heart-rot fungus.

The mountains of the West host three of the world's four sapsuckers: the **Red-breasted Sapsucker**, the **Red-naped Sapsucker**, and the **Williamson's Sapsucker**. All these species favor quaking aspen for nest excavation. Sapsuckers are highly specialized medium-size woodpeckers that drill rows of wells in trees where they harvest sap and the insects attracted to, and trapped in, the sap. To take advantage of this food source, Sapsuckers have short tongues equipped with a brushlike tip for collecting sap.

The Red-breasted and the Red-naped Sapsuckers of Western North America and the Yellow-bellied Sapsuckers of the East are very closely related and were considered one species until 1983. They share similar size and most behaviors, including calling and drumming. Although each has its specific markings, in general the amount of red increases and the amount of white decreases from east to west. Where their ranges overlap, they hybridize, resulting in various combinations of markings.

The Red-breasted Sapsucker is the westernmost of the three and breeds from southeast Alaska to northern California, from the moist coniferous forests of the coast to mixed forests at over 9,500 feet. This species prefers to forage in old growth when it is available and is the most likely of the three to drill its sap wells in conifers.

The Red-naped Sapsucker breeds throughout drier western forests of the Rocky Mountains and east of the Cascade Crest.

Within this habitat, it prefers emergent growth and stands with a significant portion of broadleaf trees, particularly quaking aspen. Some aspen stands in the Cascades may house this species and Red-breasted Sapsuckers, with hybrids between them. The Red-naped is migratory, wintering south of its breeding range in the Southwest and into Mexico.

Although it prefers to nest in aspen, the Williamson's Sapsucker requires mixed conifer forests. The mix of tree species varies—in the Pacific Northwest its presence appears to correlate closely to that of western larch while it is frequently associated with Douglas-fir in Colorado. Its relative and occasional neighbor, the Red-naped Sapsucker, might nest in the same stand of aspen, but the Red-naped will select a tree bordering its preferred deciduous feeding area while the Williamson's will choose one that is adjacent to conifers. Abandoned Williamson's Sapsucker nests are utilized by mountain bluebirds, mountain chickadees, and other secondary and weak cavity nesters.

Williamson's Sapsuckers get their food from conifers, and during the nesting period they glean ants from their trunks and branches. Throughout the remainder of the year they depend upon the sap licked from wells they drill into the vascular tissues of trees. When trees are leafless, sapsuckers feed from the xylem cells that transport water and minerals from the roots to the rest of the tree, and, when the tree later leafs out, from the richer phloem cells which carry sugars from the leaves. (Xylem sap contains only 2 to 3 percent sucrose, while the phloem sap is usually more than 10 percent and can be as high as 20 to 25 percent sucrose.) They usually drill a grid of shallow wells in damaged conifers. Once they create a well, they visit it periodically for fresh sap and trapped insects and reuse it in successive years. This sapsucker is considered a keystone species for both mixed conifer-deciduous and open conifer forests because so many other species in these ecosystems utilize its wells and cavities.

The final days of March in the Cascades, Sierra Nevada, and Rockies see the arrival of the West's spring migrants, and the Williamson's Sapsucker is among the first. Traveling north from the southwestern United States and Mexico, it enters a much different climate. With snow still on the ground, this colorful and noisy woodpecker identifies suitable breeding sites in middle- to high-elevation open coniferous forests from British Columbia to California and from Montana to New Mexico; it announces spring with its characteristic calls and drumming. Males arrive first to

A failed egg is carried out of the nest cavity by a female Williamson's Sapsucker.

establish a territory. The females arrive one to two weeks later. Within three weeks of the females' arrival, pairs of Williamson's (though most of the work is done by the males) begin to excavate cavities. Pair bonds last for only one breeding season.

Cheeur is the most common of several Williamson's vocalizations, and it might be repeated in succession up to fifteen times. This call is used for territorial displays and announcements, pair formation and contact, and even as an alarm call. It is the call most often heard in conjunction with drumming. The drumming consists of one or more steady rolls of taps followed by three or four loud taps at irregular intervals. This drumming differs from that of the other sapsuckers in its more rapid roll and longer pause before and between the final taps. Drumming, or tattooing, is used primarily for communication with other members of the species. It is exercised predominantly by males during pair formation and takes place most often in the early morning.

The Williamson's is slightly larger than the other three sapsuckers, but the most striking difference is the dramatic contrast in plumage between the male and female. The sexes look so different that they were considered to be separate species until the observation of a mated pair in 1873. The male is mostly black with white masking markings, a white wing patch, and a red throat patch, while the female is almost completely dingy brown with black and white barring on the back. The only shared feature is a yellow belly. Two subspecies are recognized: the Williamson's in the western part of the range has a bill that is slightly longer, broader, and deeper than its counterpart in the eastern part of the range.

Like other woodpeckers, the Williamson's Sapsucker is fastidious about its nesting environment. While observing a nest in the eastern Cascades, I was struck by this bird's dedication to keeping the site clean. Whenever the parents came in to bring food, they always left with waste, which was not casually dropped outside the cavity but was laboriously carried bill-full by bill-full and deposited in another cavity in a tree several hundred feet away. This exceptional dedication was impressive, but witnessing the female carrying a failed egg in her bill and carefully disposing of it was startling. Whether this behavior results from a preference for a clean environment or a desire to make the nest tree more difficult for predators to find, it benefits the Williamson's, which, unlike most other cavity nesters, often nests in the same tree, although not necessarily the same cavity, for several years in a row.

Williamson's Sapsucker parents share the incubation, brooding, and feeding of young before the male departs, which is normally one or two days before the young fledge. Unique among ant-eating birds, they will bring mouths and throats full of live whole ants, rather than swallowing and regurgitating them for the young as other woodpeckers do. Young are able to gain their independence very quickly after fledging, as ant gleaning is an easy skill to master.

In addition to being a keystone species, this bird is considered an indicator species of mixed conifer-deciduous forests and open conifer forests in the United States and of old-growth larch forests in British Columbia. Populations of Williamson's Sapsucker have declined throughout their range since 1982, with populations in the Pacific Northwest taking the biggest hit. The decline is thought to be a result of forestry practices that have eliminated snags and suppressed fires.

Periodic fire benefits all woodpeckers, but perhaps none more than the **Black-backed Woodpecker**. On a trip to northern California, I was intrigued to find Black-backed Woodpeckers nesting at 6,700 feet in a live lodgepole pine in the Sierra Nevada at Yuba Pass. The elevation did not surprise me, since several other boreal (circumpolar forests of Canada and Alaska) forest species, such as the Boreal Owl and the Three-toed Woodpecker, are found in higher elevations of the mixed coniferous forest and even subalpine forests, with stunted trees, wet openings, thin soils, and cold winters that mimic boreal habitat. My surprise was due to the lack of recently burned trees anywhere nearby. As I watched these birds bring food to their young, I was also struck by the fact that the prey was often spiders rather than the beetle larvae offerings I had seen delivered to nests in burned areas. The lodgepole pine is a fire-adapted tree, and the habitat was relatively open with wide distribution of tree sizes, so perhaps a fire had occurred here in the past. I wondered how long a species at the edge of its range could hang on in less than ideal habitat. Two days later, as I drove to the airport, smoke wafted over the valley below. A forest fire had erupted nearby. The young Black-backed Woodpeckers that were about to fledge would have an easier time than their parents had.

Although the landscape in the wake of a fire seems barren and tragic, for the Black-backed Woodpecker and several other

A White-headed Woodpecker holds his body away from a pine cone to avoid soiling his feathers with sap as he extracts the seeds.

species of birds, forest fires set the stage for a new beginning, as overnight a previously challenging landscape is transformed into ideal habitat for them.

From their sooty black plumage to their preferred prey to the way they hunt, Black-backed Woodpeckers are peculiarly adapted to fill the niche between the scorching flames and the emerald leaves of new forest growth. In the absence of fires, these birds are spread thinly across the landscape, feeding upon what food they can find. Their breeding range closely matches the distribution of boreal forests and northern mountain coniferous forests. The species of conifer seems to make very little difference to their distribution. They are irruptive—meaning that their population will suddenly increase—in areas of natural disturbances, usually burns.

Wood-boring beetles assail burned trees almost as soon as the flames subside, with most of the adults from first eggs emerging between two and three years later. Black-backed Woodpeckers arrive at burns within a month of the fire, feeding on the beetle larvae and some adults. By the time all the young beetles have emerged four years after the fire, the woodpeckers have often moved on to other areas.

A month after a forest fire in Okanogan County, Washington, I caught a glimpse of an ebony flash with a golden highlight darting to a burned ponderosa pine. Shifting black bark revealed a chisel-like bill. The Black-backed Woodpecker pecked and drilled the tough black skin of the tree, pursuing the hidden wood-boring beetle larvae. Intent upon a meal, it lunged forward and probed the wood with its long, sensitive, barbed tongue, speared a grub, and pulled it into its bill.

Most woodpeckers work nervously, shifting from tree to tree, alert and prepared to flee at the slightest disturbance, but the Black-backed works methodically, mostly on tree trunks, prying the bark free with its bill or drilling into the wood, slowly moving around the trunk to avoid missing any prized larvae. In the process, huge patches of pale yellow wood are left to dry and bleach in the sun. Sometimes a trunk is stripped entirely bare of bark by this meticulous bird. Birders are often struck by how tame the Black-backed seems; although aware of their presence, it moves slowly up the tree or flits over to an adjacent tree rather

Although this young Black-backed Woodpecker peeks from a cavity in a live tree, they usually nest in dead, burnt trees.

than fleeing, offering birders a rare opportunity to observe up-close for a prolonged period.

Because the Black-backed Woodpecker is reportedly rare, I was not surprised to see neither it nor its carpentry during my first twenty years of exploring the mountains of the West.

Opposite: The Northern Pygmy-Owl's size and coloration help it blend into the mixed-forest environment where it might be mistaken for a cone on a Douglas-fir.

In recent years, however, with the increasing frequency of forest fires, I often see this woodpecker while exploring recent burns, and it has begun to seem almost common. Outbreaks of wood-boring beetles and the absence of small mammals in burned areas are important habitat elements for this species: the beetles and their larvae sustain the woodpeckers, while the

Male Three-toed Woodpeckers, like male Black-backed Woodpeckers, are distinguished from females by their golden crowns.

absence of nest predators like squirrels improves the chances of successfully raising young.

The anatomical adaptations common to all woodpeckers for foraging in wood, such as rib structure and skulls greatly modified for pounding, are exceptionally well developed in the Black-backed Woodpecker, whose preferred prey is located deep within the wood of burned trees. Another adaptation is the absence of a fourth toe (the hallux). When other species of woodpeckers drill in a tree, three toes grip the wood while they rarely engage the fourth, and it is often cramped under the leg or held out to the side. Without the hallux in the way, the Black-backed Woodpecker is able to extend its body back farther from the tree, allowing it to direct more force into its blows. This enhances its ability to drill but limits agility, making it one of the least graceful woodpeckers.

During the two to four years they spend in a burn, Black-backed Woodpeckers create new cavities every spring in which they lay their eggs and raise their young. As older nestlings come to the cavity entrance to be fed, males can be distinguished from females by the more prominent yellow on the crown, which extends forward to the eyes.

These woodpeckers' cavities often differ from those of other northern woodpeckers in the absence of bark around the cavity, which creates a platelike appearance. These cavities later serve as breeding habitat for many secondary cavity nesters, such as bluebirds, wrens, swallows, swifts, chickadees, titmice, and small owls. Unlike many woodpeckers that excavate their cavities in open forest, Black-backed Woodpeckers make their home in denser stands of trees, benefiting secondary cavity nesters that also prefer this setting.

The Black-backed Woodpecker is very vocal, with several different calls, including the *scream-rattle-snarl*, the most distinctive of all. This call is used during encounters with other woodpeckers of its own and other species, most often as an aid in establishing territory.

The **Three-toed Woodpecker** is similar in appearance to the Black-backed. Both are medium-size woodpeckers, and the males of both species possess features unique among North American woodpeckers: three toes and yellow caps on the males. The Three-toed Woodpecker sports more white in its plumage, most notably on the center of its back. Like the Black-backed Woodpecker, the Three-toed has an exceptionally reinforced skull that enables even greater pounding and drilling force.

In contrast to the noisy Black-backed, the Three-toed Woodpecker is perhaps the quietest of all woodpeckers, infrequently uttering a soft *kik*. It expresses itself with its drumming, however, more frequently than other woodpeckers.

The Three-toed's distribution is similar to that of the Black-backed, with the majority of its breeding populations in the boreal forest, but it differs in that its range is mostly limited to that of spruce forests. Its range extends farther north in the boreal forest and to higher elevations in the rainy forests of the subalpine western mountains than any other woodpecker.

Like the Black-backed, the Three-toed can be irruptive, with populations often moving south of their normal breeding range, even into cities temporarily. Unlike the Black-backed, however, the Three-toed's irruptions are not tied primarily to burns. It also responds to tree die-offs resulting from pollution and natural disturbances such as blowdowns, floods, and insect infestations.

While the Black-backed prefers feeding on wood-boring beetles, the Three-toed prefers bark beetles, including the two biggest pests of western forests: the mountain pine beetle and the spruce beetle. The primary food of Three-toed Woodpeckers in British Columbia is mountain pine beetles. In Colorado, Three-toed and other woodpeckers were shown to reduce the populations of spruce beetles, both through predation and by desiccating the trees, thereby killing some larvae and reducing the food supply of those remaining; it is now believed that Three-toed and other woodpeckers play a significant role in limiting the impact of these forest pests.

Habitat and prey specialization leave Black-backed and Three-toed Woodpeckers vulnerable to wide-scale destruction when fire suppression, cutting of old-growth habitat, or salvage logging of burned, diseased, or insect-damaged trees limit their preferred habitats.

One warm summer evening in Colorado's Rocky Mountains, while waiting near a nesting cavity in an aspen snag tucked into a mixed Douglas-fir-ponderosa pine stand, I heard a series of short, soft, low-pitched *hoots*. They seemed to come from far away, but moments later their source, a tiny owl, alighted on an aspen branch in front of me. He darted to a nearby ponderosa pine and flung himself to the underside of the highest branch. While his talons held him upside down, his wings flapped as he plucked a moth from underneath the branch with his bill. He returned to his perch, diving to his nest cavity to deliver the moth to an owlet waiting at the entrance.

The **Flammulated Owl** is the second-smallest owl in North America. Females are slightly larger but otherwise indistinguishable from males. These owls are mostly gray with black streaks and bars combined with a highly variable flammulated (reddish) wash. They have small ear tufts that are usually flattened but can stand up dramatically when the owls are roosting during the day or when they feel threatened enough to go into their cryptic or "broken branch" posture. In this posture they—like other owls with ear tufts—lengthen their bodies and close their eyes to slits, instantly resembling a branch or broken piece of wood. Their long, pointed wings cover their small tail when perched, and their feet are small and unfeathered. When open, their black eyes, unique among small owls in North America, make them hard to confuse with any other owl. When in their cryptic posture with their eyes closed, they could be mistaken for the much grayer and larger Whiskered Screech-Owl.

Highly migratory, Flammulated Owls inhabit western North America only during the breeding season, roughly May to October. During this time, they are found in mountain pine regions in southern British Columbia, eastern Washington and Oregon, and into California, Nevada, and Utah, as well as in areas of Colorado, New Mexico, Arizona, Idaho, and Montana. Very little is known about their range outside the breeding season, but it is thought that they winter from as far north as the southwestern United States to as far south as El Salvador.

Flammulated Owls feed upon moths, their primary prey during the early part of the breeding season, as well as upon beetles, crickets, grasshoppers, and other insects. This diet necessitates the long migration they undertake each year. Flammulated Owls have been documented preying upon other birds and rodents, but that is probably very rare behavior. Having held both young Flammulated Owls and young Ferruginous Pygmy-Owls in my hands, I can attest the difference in talons is dramatic; the Pygmy-Owl's talons slid into my flesh like a hot blade on butter, while the Flammulated Owl's talons felt like the claws of a lizard, prickly but harmless.

Freezing evenings are common and snowstorms possible in late April and early May in the Flammulated Owl's mountain

Ear tufts raised in an attempt to blend in with the tree bark, an adult Flammulated Owl peers from her cavity.

habitat, and catching enough insect prey can be a challenge then. During this time, the Flammulated's hunger is primarily satisfied by Noctuids (owlet moths) and Geometrids, the only two moth families capable of flying in subfreezing temperatures.

Flammulated Owls hunt exclusively at night, with peaks one hour after sunset and one hour before sunrise. A visual hunter, this owl locates its prey with its sharp black eyes. While watching from a perch, usually within the canopy of older coni- fers, the Flammulated Owl will move its head horizontally and vertically, apparently in an effort to judge the distance of its prey before attacking. It then swoops in to pluck its insect prey from pine needles, bark, or branches or the forest floor before return- ing to its hunting perch.

Unlike other insectivorous birds that carry mouths full of insects to their young, Flammulated Owls are single-prey load- ers, bringing one item at a time and making frequent nest visits.

One year after a fire hit this ponderosa pine forest, wildflowers and woodpecker excavations signal recovery.

Owlet moths, like the one captured by this Flammulated Owl, are able to fly in subfreezing temperatures and are thus this owl's most important food item early in the breeding season.

Observing a pair of owls one evening near Colorado Springs, I was struck by the frenetic pace of hunting and food delivery. During the first hour after sunset, both owls were hunting and the young were fed every few minutes.

Other North American forest owls have short wings optimized for maneuverability between and around trees, but the Flammulated Owl has long wings, possibly an adaptation for its long migration. The loss in maneuverability resulting from these longer wings could be one reason that this owl prefers to hunt in the forest canopy, in open spaces above shrubs, on the ground, and at the edges of the forest. Its favorite place to hunt seems to be within the crown of the oldest trees in the vicinity.

Within its range, the Flammulated Owl prefers ridge tops, slopes, and adjacent plateaus of older mixed ponderosa pine and Douglas-fir with a shrubby or grassy understory. While it is most common in ponderosa pine forests with Douglas-fir, gambel oak, and quaking aspen, it can also be found in pinyon-juniper woodlands. For unknown reasons, it avoids pure ponderosa pine stands.

Old-growth forests are the preferred habitat as they usually contain large lightning-damaged snags that may contain cavities and other large trees for foraging, calling, and daytime roosting. Old-growth ponderosa pine and Douglas-fir mix often provides more open habitat, featuring grassy or shrub understories for foraging and multitudes of the moths favored as prey by this owl.

Nest sites are often situated in areas with high insect density. The nests are usually old woodpecker holes in pines and sometimes aspens, particularly those created by Northern Flickers and Pileated Woodpeckers, although cavities created by Sapsuckers, Hairy Woodpeckers, and White-headed Woodpeckers are utilized as well. The availability of woodpecker cavities is probably a limiting factor to populations throughout the Flammulated Owl's breeding range.

Unlike many migratory birds, mated pairs often return to the same territory and mate again. For some reason, males outnumber females. If a female's mate fails to return, she will usually relocate and mate with a male in a neighboring territory. Males on the other hand always return to defend and advertise from their existing territory even if their mate does not return. It is common to find males without mates calling throughout the breeding season. Some researchers speculate that breeding

The Northern Pygmy-Owl is small enough to perch on the trunk of a quaking aspen.

males' wanderings the year before may familiarize them with the females in neighboring territories. These territories are usually twenty-five to fifty acres and do not overlap with the territories of neighboring males, although an aspen grove might contain the nests of two males whose territories start there and head in opposite directions.

Three Flammulated Owl chicks wait to be banded by a researcher.

A brilliantly colored male Williamson's Sapsucker brings live ants to his young.

and sound remarkably like the call of the much larger Long-eared Owl. The primary call is described as a single, flat, short *hoot.* Different males sing at slightly different frequencies, and when an intruder comes close the calls become much more hoarse. When humans are present, these owls decrease the amplitude of their calls, creating the impression that they are farther away. As birders know, this owl is hard enough to locate without such a misleading call. Mated males sing throughout the early part of the breeding season but less frequently after that. Unmated males may sing incessantly throughout summer. Females' calls have a higher pitch than those of males and are frequently used to solicit food from the male. These owls have several additional calls, including loud shrieks emitted while flying at the heads of intruders, including humans, who approach too closely to nests.

The Flammulated Owl is considered an indicator species for open, large-diameter ponderosa pine habitat. Within such habitats that meet its nesting and prey requirements, the owl can be quite common. Its specific habitat requirements, low productivity rate, long migration, and dependence on commercially valuable timber leave populations vulnerable to large-scale declines. Its survival is heavily dependent on forestry practices and policies in North America, Mexico, and Central America. While it has so far survived a period of heavy logging in North America, its wintering range is currently under tremendous pressure.

For Flammulated Owls, the presence of dead standing trees with woodpecker holes is a critical habitat element, and the removal of these for firewood or during logging operations could threaten populations. Nest-hole competition from nonnative starlings and other threats to populations of cavity-creating woodpeckers could also have devastating impacts on populations of Flammulated Owls.

Despite preferring old growth, Flammulated Owls do not necessarily require virgin forests and may benefit from selective thinning that removes competing younger trees and retains more open stands of trees of various ages and species and a brushy or grassy understory.

Downslope from the Douglas-fir and ponderosa pine regions east of the Cascades or anywhere in California's Sierra Nevada, the precipitation decreases and only extremely fire-resistant and drought-tolerant trees thrive. In much of the West this zone is dominated by ponderosa pine.

During courtship the male typically shows several cavities to the female, who apparently selects the one to use. From the period of courtship, production of a small clutch, and incubation until the owlets are almost two weeks old, the male will feed the female and owlets, but after that the parents share the feeding duties.

Flammulated Owls are famous for their ventriloquial calls, which are surprisingly low pitched for such a small owl

Although I photographed the **White-headed Woodpecker** in the mixed-conifer area of Yuba Pass in the Sierra, it is most closely associated with ponderosa pine and attains its greatest densities in areas where two or more species of pine with large seed-laden cones coexist. Since ponderosa pines have highly variable cone crops, the presence of multiple pine species reduces the risk of food shortage. Other trees with seeds of interest to this bird include sugar pine, Jeffrey pine, western white pine, and Coulter pine. Forests dominated by species with smaller cones, such as lodgepole pine, knobcone pine, and singleleaf pinyon pine, are avoided. In central and southern California where Coulter pinecones are an important food source, the White-headed Woodpecker has adapted to the large spiky cones of this tree by developing a bill significantly longer than that of its northern counterparts.

This woodpecker can be found from south-central British Columbia in mountainous coniferous forests, east of the Cascade Crest in Washington and Oregon, in the mountains of eastern Oregon and western Idaho, in California along the Coastal Range, and through the Sierra Nevada (more common on the west slope) into western Nevada. Throughout its range, the elevation it inhabits varies by latitude, from below 2,300

Open stands of mature ponderosa pine provide nesting areas for White-headed Woodpeckers.

The male White-headed Woodpecker can be differentiated from the female by the red feathers on the back of his head.

feet in British Columbia, to as high as 7,550 feet in southern California. It is unknown why many areas with healthy stands of ponderosa pine, such as the Rocky Mountains, are not inhabited by this woodpecker.

White-headed Woodpeckers harvest pine seeds in fall and winter; larval insects, ants, and sap make up the majority of their diet during the rest of the year. They create their own sap wells in the form of regular horizontal rings around small trees but also raid the wells of sapsuckers, such as the Williamson's and the Red-naped. Because they forage visually, it has been proposed that their white head is an adaptation that reflects light into cracks and crevices as an aid in the search for food.

Unlike its close relative the Hairy Woodpecker, the White-headed tends to forage on the outer bark, needles, and cones of pine and other trees. Its foraging technique involves superficial tapping and flaking of the bark, and it creates much less noise than the Hairy. Because it makes so little noise, this woodpecker can be difficult to find. However, when it makes its contact call to its mate, its distinctive *pee-dink* can make it easier to locate.

Watching this bird with its black belly and white head held far from the bark, its legs spread as it sidled down a ponderosa pine in Washington State's eastern Cascade Mountains, I laughed and thought, *This looks like a crab, not a woodpecker.* Like other woodpeckers, the White-headed normally scales a tree with its body held close to the tree for support, but in this situation it had reason to be cautious as it was approaching a sticky sap well and did not care to soil its feathers. When White-headeds drill into unopened pinecones in pursuit of seeds, they employ similar stances, sometimes hanging acrobatically from the bottom of the cone, sometimes in a push-up-like posture above the cone, but always awkwardly holding their bodies away from sticky cones. After pecking a pinecone open, they carry the seeds to a hard piece of wood, which they use as an anvil to pound open the hull and reach the nutritious morsel within.

This medium-size woodpecker is roughly the same size as the Hairy Woodpecker, but the two species look different in other respects. Both male and female White-headed Woodpeckers possess white heads and mostly black bodies. The male has a red patch on the back of his head, and the fledglings of both sexes have a red patch on their forehead that fades as they mature.

White-headed Woodpeckers nest in stumps, snags, and the dead portions of live trees; lack of suitable cavity sites appears to be one of the greatest restrictions to their population size. Birders and photographers are usually surprised to find them nesting much lower than most other North American woodpeckers, often less than ten feet off the ground.

Considering the great physical effort required to excavate a nest cavity, it is remarkable that these birds will often near completion on several cavities before one is finished. Although a new cavity is usually created every year, sometimes a pair will reuse one from the previous year. Mountain bluebirds, pygmy nuthatches, and other secondary cavity nesters that prefer more open forests use their abandoned cavities.

The White-headed Woodpecker and Flammulated Owl are both indicator species for old-growth ponderosa pine habitat. Unfortunately, White-headed Woodpecker populations from British Columbia to Oregon are threatened due to forest fragmentation, clear-cutting, snag removal, and fire suppression. Northern populations in Oregon and Washington have been hit particularly hard. Like the Northern Pygmy-Owl, the White-headed Woodpecker is vulnerable to forest fragmentation because it does not migrate and requires linked habitat. Unlike the Pygmy-Owl, the White-headed benefits little from clear-cuts, although natural or prescribed burns or thinnings that attempt to replicate natural fires can improve habitat by removing competing small trees, fire-susceptible trees, and thick understories, as long as an abundance of large snags and large cone-producing trees remains.

Prescribed burns, selective thinning, and other progressive forestry practices are gaining wider acceptance in the management of ponderosa pine forests. In addition, some conservation organizations are working to protect and connect old-growth habitat in the Pacific Northwest to reduce fragmentation, to the benefit of all plants and animals, including nonmigratory birds of this region, such as Northern Pygmy Owls and White-headed Woodpeckers.

4

Western Oak Woodlands

Oak woodlands are a dry, open ecosystem with a grassy understory; they form a wide swath along the foothills of California's mountain ranges just below the ponderosa pine zone, particularly along the western slope of the Sierra Nevada, the northern Coast Range, and the southern Cascades. Dry oak habitat can also be found throughout much of Oregon's Willamette Valley and on the east side of Washington's southern Cascades, where it is interspersed with the lowest-elevation ponderosas, just before they give way to shrub-steppe. In this habitat's highest elevations, oak is often mixed with ponderosa pine and other pines, in a system often referred to as oak-pine before the dry, thin soil challenges the shorter taproots of the faster-growing evergreens.

Small, isolated groups of red-barked ponderosa pines dotted the hillsides, groves of gnarly branched Oregon white oak decorated the valleys, and tall, thirsty black cottonwoods hugged a stream I passed while hiking in the Cascade foothills of south-central Washington. I expected to see flycatchers and swallows hunting insects on the wing (flycatching), but I did not expect such graceful feats from the ungainly woodpecker for which I was searching. My first field observation of **Lewis's Woodpeckers** included many surprises. At least half a dozen large dark birds were in view at the tops of burned oak trees along the stream. Periodically one would launch, its long pointed wings and tail spread out, gliding through the air, making soft but quick turns, subtle drops in elevation, and light upward jerks in pursuit of insects before returning to its perch. These birds lacked the undulating flight, aggressive territorial interactions, and pursuit of insects or larvae on the trunks and branches of trees characteristic of woodpeckers; when returning from a sortie for insects, they perched horizontally on the branches rather than vertically against the trunk as most woodpeckers do.

My companion was unimpressed because to her, from the distance, they looked like crows. Her observation put her in good company though; after discovering this bird in 1805 on the Lewis and Clark Voyage of Discovery, Meriwether Lewis wrote, "I saw a black woodpecker (or crow) today, about the size of the lark woodpecker as black as a crow," and added, "it is a distinct species of woodpecker; it has a long tail and flies a good deal like a jay bird."

The Lewis's is a large woodpecker, slightly shorter but with a heavier build and longer wings than the Northern Flicker, which Lewis referred to as the "lark woodpecker." To facilitate aerial pursuit of insects, the Lewis's Woodpecker has the largest gape (mouth opening) of any woodpecker. Lewis did a wonderful job of describing this bird: "[A]round the base of the beak including

Opposite: Wild currant berries and other fruits and nuts are common components of the omnivorous Lewis's Woodpecker's diet.

A male Acorn Woodpecker makes a rare trip to the woodland floor to search among the Garry oak leaves for acorns.

the eye and a small part of the throat is of a fine crimson red. The neck and as low as the croop in front is of an iron grey. The belly and breast is a curious mixture of blood reed [red] which has much the appearance of having been artificially painted or stained of that colour. The read reather [red rather] predominates. The top of the head, back, sides, upper surface of the wings and tail are black with a gossey [glossy] tint of green in a certain exposure to the light." Lewis was right in noting "this bird in its actions when flying resembles the small red-headed woodpecker common to the Atlantic states; it's note also somewhat resembles this bird." Today the Red-headed Woodpecker is recognized as the Lewis's Woodpecker's closest living relative. Fittingly, the bird was named after Meriwether Lewis.

A quiet bird, the Lewis's Woodpecker calls regularly only during the breeding season, and drumming is undertaken only by the male and only during courtship. For most woodpeckers, drumming is the primary method used in attracting a mate; for the Lewis's the primary call serves this purpose. As Meriwether Lewis noted, the call heard most often is similar to that of the Red-headed Woodpecker and consists of a loud, harsh *churr* given several times in quick succession. The drumming is short, weak, and of medium speed and is often followed by several individual taps, reminiscent of sapsuckers.

The Lewis's is relatively common in some areas of its range and rare in others. It is perhaps most common in northeast Arizona and on the eastern slope of the Cascade Mountains in Washington and Oregon during summer and in northern New Mexico, southern Colorado, northern California, and southern Oregon during winter. This species is often migratory, breeding in open high-elevation pine forests, pine-oak woodlands, and low-elevation riparian cottonwood stands when its primary food is insects; in winter, it travels to sources of acorns, nuts, fruit, and corn. The birds in the northern part of the range are the most migratory, with many in British Columbia, Washington, and Oregon dispersing south and west by early September. That said, in places such as Fort Simcoe in Yakima County, Washington, if the native Garry oaks have a strong crop of acorns—a frequent biennial occurrence—breeding Lewis's Woodpeckers may stay for winter and are often joined by other Lewis's Woodpeckers that migrate to partake of this bonanza. Most arrive back at their breeding grounds by early May.

Open areas with recent burns of pine or oak and open pine stands with brushy understories, downed decaying trees, and solitary snags located adjacent to water represent premium Lewis's Woodpecker breeding habitat, as these situations are rife with flying insects. Since the Lewis's pursues insects from the air, perches that are in or bordering an open area are important habitat elements.

Although not a cooperative breeder, the Lewis's will often nest closer to others of the same species than any other woodpecker; sometimes two pairs will even nest in the same tree. I have witnessed approximately six pairs nesting along a two-mile stretch of a stream in an oak burn, with nests within thirty yards of each other. During several days of observation, I did not witness any aggressive or competitive encounters among these birds. That said, the Lewis's is territorial and aggressive toward other species of woodpeckers, with a particularly vehement reaction to Acorn Woodpeckers, which are competitors for food and nesting space.

The Lewis's often caches food, particularly during fall and winter. Although protective of the stored food, Lewis's Woodpeckers are not at all competitive or possessive over the sources of this food, easily sharing a favorite oak tree or berry bush. Acorns, berries, and other crops are usually taken from the tree or bush and almost never salvaged from the ground. Rather than storing acorns whole like the Acorn Woodpecker does, the Lewis's takes acorns, nuts, fruits, and even insects to a frequently used and flat, hard site atop a snag, where it breaks its selections into pieces before consuming them or storing them in bark or crevices. During winter, the stashed pieces of food are either consumed or turned and moved to new crevices, a process that probably reduces fungal growth.

The Lewis's is a very weak excavator. As a result, it favors habitats with trees in an advanced state of decay so it can drill cavities more easily, and it tends to reuse its own nest cavities from the previous year. It sometimes takes over cavities previously, or even currently, being used by other birds, and it also will use nest boxes. The importance of well-decayed snags to its habitat cannot be overemphasized, though, as the cavities in these snags are also used as roost sites throughout the year. If situated in the open, snags make good hunting platforms, too.

Upon fledging, Lewis's Woodpeckers lack flying skills and often stay at the nest tree for several days, which leaves them vulnerable to predation by kestrels and various hawks and owls.

These youngsters look quite different from the adults, with highly variable brown markings instead of a red face and breast.

Lewis's Woodpeckers are the shyest woodpeckers; they often avoid human structures and reportedly are quick to abandon nests that are approached too closely by humans. Birders and photographers should watch from a distance of at least fifty feet and should observe and photograph through digiscopes and the longest of lenses behind blinds. If the bird does not return to the nest with food within a few minutes, the viewer is too close.

This bird's population has declined 53 percent in the last forty years. Due to its cyclical presence in many parts of its range, particularly in winter, it is difficult to be certain of the causes or the extent of its decline. The primary cause is probably the dramatic decrease in open ponderosa pine habitat throughout

Where this open ponderosa pine forest transitions into oak woodlands, Acorn, Lewis's, and Nuttall's Woodpeckers, as well as Western Screech-Owls and Northern Pygmy-Owls, all find breeding habitat.

British Columbia, Washington, Oregon, and Arizona. This decline is the result of fire suppression, intensive grazing, and selective logging with replanting of closely spaced seedlings, all of which play roles in the conversion of this habitat to one featuring tight stands of small ponderosa pine and invading, faster-growing, less fire-resistant, more shade-tolerant Douglas-fir. In eastern Or-

egon, for example, as much as 92 to 98 percent of open ponderosa pine habitat has been lost. Nest cavity competition from nonnative European starlings and pesticides in the environment have also been cited as possible contributors to this bird's decline.

Yet the Lewis's Woodpecker is compatible with sustainable forestry. If pines are thinned and tall, large-diameter decayed

With a bill full of fresh insects from a fly-catching sortie, a Lewis's Woodpecker prepares to return to the nest.

snags are left for nest sites, roosts, and insect-hunting perches, open parklike stands of ponderosa pine can be created and will improve the breeding habitat. Fortunately, due to the presence of mature cottonwoods and cultivated corn in agricultural areas, the Lewis's Woodpecker has enjoyed a small expansion of its range onto the plains of southeast Colorado.

California enjoys more than twenty oak species, and several animals take advantage of their acorn bounty. No species in this habitat, however, has a tighter association with acorns and oak woodland habitat than does the **Acorn Woodpecker**.

Waka, waka, waka rang out all around me as Acorn Woodpeckers greeted members of their colony passing by on acorn-gathering missions in an oak grove near Palo Alto, California. Most woodpeckers are solitary and aggressively protect stored food, but here several woodpeckers worked side by side to lodge freshly picked acorns in holes they had drilled in the bark of a large oak tree. These birds appeared to dance with each other on the face of the tree, as an acorn was placed into a hole, only to be retrieved when it proved too easy to pull out. After several attempts at finding an appropriate-size hole, they would finally succeed when the acorn required several stiff hits to push it tightly into its hold. I observed no aggression until a ground squirrel attempted to steal an acorn from a hole and five Acorn Woodpeckers descended upon it like an avalanche of stones, attacking with their long bills until it scampered away.

Acorn Woodpeckers are highly social, living in cohesive units and cooperating in food storage and breeding. These medium-size, clownish-looking woodpeckers occur discontinuously among oak trees in far western North America from northwestern Oregon through southern California, and from Arizona through Central America, and one small isolated population occurs in south-central Washington. They can be found among pines and redwoods and in riparian areas, as long as oaks are present. Two subspecies are found in the United States, with western populations possessing longer bills than southwestern populations.

Half the diet of Acorn Woodpeckers is acorns, despite the fact that insects are this bird's favorite food. Insects are difficult for these nonmigratory birds to find in winter, when adult insects are dormant and larvae are hidden deep in trees. Most woodpeckers pursue insect larvae by drilling into the bark or wood of trees, but Acorn Woodpeckers glean insects from tree

Looking for a tight fit, an Acorn Woodpecker inserts an acorn into a hole in a granary tree.

limbs or catch them on the fly from the tree canopy, methods unlikely to secure many insects during the winter months.

A granary tree, or food storage tree full of acorns, is the best guarantee of a successful breeding season. Acorns are necessary to get these birds through winter in healthy breeding condition, and they enable parents to feed a greater percentage of nutritious insects caught in spring to their young. Studies show that two to five times as many young can fledge from groups that have acorn stores remaining.

A male sentinel for a colony of Acorn Woodpeckers flees after alerting the others to danger.

Since the size of acorn crops for each species of tree in a particular area is cyclical, populations of Acorn Woodpeckers are most resilient in regions with a greater diversity of oak species. This probably explains why they are nearly absent from Washington State, with its one native oak, while they are quite common in California, where sometimes four or five species of oak grow in a single area.

Most Acorn Woodpecker family groups have one primary and one or more secondary granary trees, each containing between a few and 50,000 holes. Large granaries are the cumulative investment of generations of woodpeckers, with each bird drilling a few holes a year, generally during winter and after filling existing holes with a successful fall harvest. Acorn Woodpeckers drill their granary holes in the thick bark of trees, without inhibiting tree growth, and fill the holes with all available nuts, including almonds, walnuts, hazelnuts, pecans, and pine nuts, in addition to acorns. Although granary storage of acorns is the rule in Oregon and California, this practice is less common in the southwestern states, where acorns are stored in natural cracks and holes in bark, and populations sometimes migrate south to find food when stores are exhausted.

Occasionally, fresh acorns are brought to an anvil—a hard

flat surface on limbs where cracks hold food in place while it is broken apart—where the shell is removed or penetrated and the meat is taken piecemeal either to be eaten or fed to the young. Stored acorns are broken at the same anvils and often are infested with insect larvae. These larvae are also consumed, but contrary to speculation it appears that the acorn meat and not the larvae motivate their storage practice.

Acorn Woodpeckers are opportunistic in their feeding habits. They consume fruit, flower nectar, eggs, sap, lizards, and insects, favoring ants, bees, and wasps. They create sap wells in spring after acorn stores have been exhausted. They space these like acorn holes but make them much shallower and smaller in diameter. Acorn Woodpeckers often visit these wells in groups and use them for several years in a row.

Acorn Woodpeckers have a complex colonial breeding structure involving one to seven related male breeders, one to

After delivering food to its nestlings, a Lewis's Woodpecker squeezes out of its cavity in a Garry oak snag.

three related egg-laying females, and up to ten male and female nonbreeding helpers that are the offspring from previous years.

Males compete to mate with females, often mating in succession and attempting to interrupt mating with other males. The females lay eggs in a common nest cavity but will remove, destroy, and even eat eggs that have been laid prior to their own first eggs. As a result, until all females in the group are actively laying eggs, no eggs will survive. The resulting parental uncertainty ensures that all adults in the group will look after the young.

When the last female or male of a breeding group dies, gangs of nonbreeding helpers of the same gender as the deceased come from outside the group to compete for the vacancies in the reproductive chain. The struggle between rival birds results in a melee of aggressive calls, chases, and physical attacks that often finds birds tangled and pecking each other's heads as they fall to the ground. Fighting can last for weeks but in the end is generally won by the largest group.

Within their own group, nonbreeding helpers are ineligible for any breeding vacancies as long as their opposite sex parent or relatives hold a breeding role, a practice which prevents incest. Helpers may remain for up to five years while looking for opportunities to become part of the breeding group of another colony.

Every Acorn Woodpecker territory contains several cavities. Some are used for night roosts, and one is used for nesting. Nests can be excavated in oak trees, cottonwoods, ponderosa pines, redwoods, and even telephone poles. Nest cavities are typically used for several consecutive years. Northern Pygmy-Owls, Flammulated Owls, and Elf Owls use the vacated cavities, and occasionally small owls, wood rats, chipmunks, and feral honeybees will usurp them. Not surprisingly, Acorn Woodpeckers are a keystone species in oak habitats.

Virtually every forested habitat in North America features a small woodpecker that can explore surfaces and capture prey inaccessible to larger woodpeckers. In most of North America, it is the Downy Woodpecker, but in western California the Downy is restricted to riparian areas, and even in these areas its populations nearly peter out in southern California. The **Nuttall's Woodpecker** seizes this niche in the oak woodlands of much of California and in riparian areas in southern California.

This woodpecker appears to bounce through the trees, rarely moving far on a particular branch or small stem before flitting to another. It might at one moment tap its bill to widen a crevice to extract an insect and, at the next moment, leap to the underside of a hanging bunch of elderberries. At other times it might race up the trunk of a tree, using its stiff tail feathers for balance like other woodpeckers, while scraping small beetles from the bark and peering into crevices before flitting to a tiny twig nearby.

The Nuttall's Woodpecker is only slightly larger than the Downy and looks quite similar. The two are best distinguished by the white barring on the Nuttall's' back versus the white midback on the Downy, as well as the greater amount of red on the crown of the male Nuttall's. Even its behaviors are similar to the Downy's, and it is also a weak excavator, requiring trees or branches in advanced stages of decay to carve a nest for laying eggs.

For maintenance of populations of Acorn Woodpeckers, Nuttall's Woodpeckers, and the entire California oak woodland habitat, oak populations must be healthy, with mature trees for nest cavities and granaries and younger trees to replace these older ones as they decay or are blown down. Unfortunately, oak regeneration is poor, due in large part to overgrazing. This has resulted in vulnerable stands of old trees with very little diversity in age.

Fortunately, both Acorn Woodpeckers and Nuttall's Woodpeckers can adapt to human presence. This provides people with the opportunity to supplement and steward habitat in the dry oak woodland region of California by planting and protecting younger oak trees, as well as protecting older trees, particularly those with dead and decaying branches and trunks in residential areas.

Opposite: Foraging more like a nuthatch than a typical woodpecker, a Nuttall's Woodpecker clings to a bunch of elderberries.

5

Grasslands and Shrub-Steppe

Grassland and shrub-steppe habitats are found in the rain shadows of the West's major mountain ranges. The rain shadows rob moisture from Washington's Columbia Basin, Oregon's high desert, California's Central Valley, the Southwest's Great Basin, and the Great Plains, punishing them with scorching heat and frequent winds, preventing the establishment of trees, except along rivers and other waterways. The grasslands lie slightly higher than the drier and warmer shrub-steppe. Although these areas might not seem to offer ideal habitat for what we think of as tree-loving birds, they offer prime habitat for specialized owls that hunt the open country on the wing.

The **Short-eared Owl** is a medium-size owl that can be found throughout the northern parts of North America in grasslands, marshes, and tundra. Breeding takes place from the Arctic throughout Canada and in many of the northern states. Short-eared Owls breeding in Alaska and much of Canada migrate south during winter, when they can be found in all the Lower 48 states.

The plumage of Short-eared Owls resembles the dry grass in which they live. The back and wings are mottled brown, while the breast is rusty white with vertical streaks of dark straw brown. The head is large and round with a distinct facial disk and small ear tufts that are occasionally erected from the center of the forehead. Males are slightly smaller than females but are better distinguished by their lighter color overall. The Short-eared Owl is similar in shape to the smaller Long-eared Owl. During the infrequent times when the two share a winter roost, the Long-eared Owl is easily distinguished by its distinctive long ear tufts, although in flight, when the tufts are down against the head, they are much more difficult to identify.

Northern harrier hawks are more often confused with Short-eared Owls, as they breed in the same habitats and often hunt at the same time. In flight, the harrier can be distinguished by its white rump patch and longer tail, as well as by its wings, which are usually held horizontally; the Short-eared Owl's wings, like the owl itself, rise and fall more frequently.

Although typically crepuscular (active at twilight), Short-eared Owls will hunt any time of the day or night. On consecutive days, I have watched them refrain from hunting until dusk one day, then hunt most of the afternoon on the following day on the same hunting grounds. Potential prey is most active, and competition from diurnal (active in the daylight) raptors such as harriers is less intense, during those twilight hours. They may continue hunting into the day if they have not captured enough food.

Short-eared Owls are closely associated with populations

Opposite: Tilting its head from side to side, a Short-eared Owl pinpoints its prey in the grass below.

Although it hunts in open country, the Long-eared Owl is most frequently seen roosting within the dense branches of pine trees.

of small mammals, such as voles, and are often extremely no-madic in pursuit of them during the winter months. They take other small mammals and birds occasionally, and like other owls of the open country, most of their hunting occurs on the wing. They travel close to the ground, and their keen sense of hearing and silent wings allow them to locate prey even in flight.

Because they live in the open, Short-eared Owls are vulner-able to predation by domestic cats and dogs, wild carnivores, and raptors. Populations have plummeted in the past forty years, falling by 71 percent. The open habitat they require is often lost to agriculture, grazing, recreation, and housing and resort developments. Some conservation programs have been effective in restoring habitat but population recovery has oc-curred only when they preserve large blocks of habitat of more than 2,470 acres.

Short-eareds nest in a variety of grassy habitats where the grass is tall enough to hide a brooding female. The female scratches a nest bowl directly on the ground and usually lines it with grasses and downy feathers, providing one of the few examples of an owl creating its own nest. Nest sites are almost always on dry ground and often on a ridge, knoll, or hummock, particularly in moist environments, and are occasionally reused. Sometimes nests are found in close proximity to one another, probably a function of available prey, nesting cover, and a suitably dry site.

In winter Short-eared Owls that breed in the Arctic and most of those that breed in Canada migrate south. They are often found in grassy estuarine habitat in places such as Wash-ington's Skagit River Delta and British Columbia's Boundary Bay, where they join peregrine falcons, rough-legged hawks, northern harriers, and Snowy Owls hunting the open expanses before returning north to their harsher breeding areas.

The broad, wet grasslands of British Columbia's Boundary Bay offer the ideal setting for voles, and thus also for Short-eared Owls. Bathed in low winter light one January afternoon, northern harriers glided and sliced through the air above the golden-brown expanse. The light faded, but none of the Short-eared Owls I was hoping to photograph appeared. Suddenly, as I was about to put my gear away and give up for the day, owls rose from the grass that had camouflaged them so well. They followed an irregular, mothlike course through the air, bounc-ing up before quickly falling, and hovering before plunging into tufts of grass, then rising up again to continue their hunt. The

Barn Owls are most commonly encountered in barns and other man-made structures.

harriers initially confronted their neighbors but then retreated to their own grassy hideouts. Dusk and the dark in these grass-lands belong to the Short-eared Owl.

During winter, large communal roosts of up to 200 Short-eared Owls can occur. I have observed a winter roost of 15

Elevated perches are a critical element of Burrowing Owl habitat.

in the meadow. Occasionally, if winter roosts provide plenty of food, these owls will stay and breed there.

Befitting a vulnerable ground-nesting bird, Short-eared Owls are the least vocal owls, with most calling limited to courtship. Courtship calls begin in February or March when many are still on their winter grounds. The primary call is *voo-hoo-hoo-hoo-hoo.*

Late in winter as communal roosts break up, males often vocalize a second song as they begin performing their "sky dances." A male flies perhaps 200 to 300 feet up in a spiral, then swoops down while slapping his wings together on the downward stroke several times. He then ascends again in tight circles to as high as 500 feet, at which time he either soars stationary in the wind or flies forward with his wings and tail fanned out while calling *hoo-hoo-hoo-hoo-hoo-hoo* before making another shallow swoop with more wing claps. During this display, the female perches on the ground, calling. The male repeats this sequence several times before joining her on the ground and approaching while rocking side to side. After the male passes, the female sometimes chases him away, but usually they follow each other head to tail into taller grass where it is believed they mate.

Several typical features are particularly pronounced in owls that hunt on the wing. Like many other owls, flight sounds of the Short-eared Owl are muffled by several feather adaptations on its wings that absorb sound. The most distinctive feature of the Short-eared Owl is its long wings, which dwarf the rest of its body, hinting at an extremely low wing load (the amount of weight distributed across the surface area of the wing, expressed in grams per centimeter). Its lower wing loading provides the Short-eared Owl with exceptional buoyancy in flight, allowing it to fly slowly and silently, avoiding detection while its keen hearing pinpoints voles moving through the grass. At the same time, this buoyancy and the owl's agility allow it to stop and hover midflight or change course in an instant.

Low wing loading is of great benefit to owls that hunt in the open: since very few perches are available from which to pounce upon their prey, they must ambush their prey from the air. The Short-eared Owl has the third-lowest wing loading among all North American owls. Not surprisingly, the two with lower

Short-eareds near Ladner, British Columbia. The owls spent the day hidden in the tall grass but dispersed one by one to hunt in separate areas at dawn and dusk. When snowfall made their camouflage less effective, they found sanctuary on small isolated spits and islands offshore and in clumps of bushes growing

Previous page: Four Short-eared Owls, with ear tufts raised, share a winter roost along a tidal flat in British Columbia.

wing loading are also owls that hunt in the unforested habitats of North America.

The lowest wing loading belongs to the **Long-eared Owl**, a medium-size relative of the Short-eared that hunts almost exclusively in the open country but roosts and nests in adjacent dense vegetation. The Long-eared Owl, also known as the "Cat Owl" or "Lesser Horned Owl," is most easily recognized by its long ear tufts, which make it look a bit like the much larger Great Horned Owl. The ear tufts have nothing to do with its ears, which, as in all owls, are slits just behind the face.

The Long-eared Owl's ear slits are covered by movable skin flaps and run nearly the length of the skull; its asymmetrical skull results in the position and orientation of the ear opening differing between left and right. This and other adaptations equip the Long-eared Owl with phenomenal directional hearing, allowing it to isolate sounds on both horizontal and vertical

The Missouri River winds through the Great Plains in Montana. Burrowing Owls take advantage of the short-grass prairie; Short-eared Owls hunt the wet areas; and Long-eared Owls take daytime cover in the trees along the riverbanks.

A Short-eared Owl stretches both legs and wings before embarking on the evening's hunt.

Trees are scarce in the shrub-steppe and grasslands of North America, but highly adaptive Great Horned Owls take advantage of shelter offered by caves and old lava tubes.

planes, a feature invaluable to birds hunting at night. The circular feather pattern around this owl's face (its facial disk) reflects sound waves toward the ear slits, enabling it to hear low- and medium-pitched sounds ten times as well as humans can.

The Long-eared Owl is found throughout much of open and lightly forested habitats in North America, from open forest habitat across much of the boreal forest and northern states, through the grasslands and shrub-steppe of the upper Midwest and inland West, and to the Sonoran Desert scrub.

For its own nests, the Long-eared Owl uses the abandoned stick nests of magpies, crows, and other birds in groves of trees or thickets; the owl itself practically disappears against pine bark or within tangles of branches. Unlike many owls, the Long-eared is not territorial, and at times the young from several nests mix together. Communal roosts are very common and can include up to a hundred birds, although two to twenty is more common.

Strictly nocturnal across most of its range, the Long-eared Owl does not leave its roost or nest to hunt small mammals until after dark. In North America this bird is a vole and mouse specialist, and populations are nomadic from year to year, depending upon the availability of its primary prey. When small mammals are not available it will take small birds.

Rats, mice, and other small rodents are the principal prey of the nocturnal **Barn Owl**, which is equipped with the second-lowest wing loading. It uses this feature to hunt the broadest range of open habitats, from city parks to farms to shrub-steppe and even deserts throughout all but some of the northernmost states.

With its taste for rats and mice, the Barn Owl is of tremendous service to people; availability of rodents and nest sites appears to be the main limiting factor to populations. When rodent prey is scarce, the Barn Owl will course low over hedges or low shrubbery at night like the Long-eared Owl to scare roosting birds and capture them when they flush. One population in southeastern Washington feeds upon the European starling, whose aggressive usurpation of cavities reduces the populations of some woodpeckers and other cavity nesters. This is also an owl that often suffers high mortality rates along highways in winter when struck by cars while hunting mice attracted to spilled grain.

The only North American owl not a member of the Strigidae family, the Barn Owl is a member of the Tytonidae family, the "monkey-faced owls." It is not surprising, then, that this medium-size owl has a light tan color unique among North

Low wing-loading allows the Barn Owl to hunt silently over fields.

American owls, small black eyes, and a distinctively heart-shaped facial disk.

Unlike the Short-eared and Long-eared Owls, whose distributions fan out from boreal forests, the Barn Owl is primarily an owl of the tropics and subtropics that has spread northward by living close to humans and taking advantage of our alterations to the environment. It seeks protected nest sites, such as caves, cliff-side holes, barns, church steeples, nest boxes, and gaps in hay bales; sometimes nests are inadvertently moved several hundred miles when hay is transported. Its adaptability has made the Barn Owl one of the most cosmopolitan of birds.

Barn Owls, Short-eared Owls, and Long-eared Owls share a common predator in the most ferocious of North American owls: the Great Horned Owl.

The **Great Horned Owl**, also known as the "Flying Tiger," is the most adaptable owl in North America, breeding in every state and province from tree line in the North to the deserts

With his ears up, head jutting forward, and throat full of air, a calling Great Horned Owl appears to pump the "hoos" out of his body with the up and down motion of his tail.

Three Burrowing Owls peer from a burrow.

of the Southwest in nearly every habitat except for dense un-broken forests.

Plumage and size vary a great deal from region to region. The darkest individuals are associated with the moist climate of the Pacific Northwest and southern Alaska. Intermediate shades are found in the Rocky Mountains, Pacific Coast, and in eastern deciduous forests. Populations in arid climates, as in the Southwest, have light plumage, and the palest, almost white individuals are found in subarctic Canada.

The Great Horned also has the widest prey base of any owl, feeding upon everything from mice and rats to skunks, marmots, and other owls, although its preferred prey consists of hares, rabbits, and small rodents. It is able to hunt skunks without consequence because of its poorly developed sense of smell.

Although their extremely soft feathers enable silent flight, Great Horned Owls do not have low wing loading. Despite this, they prefer to hunt in open or lightly forested terrain, watching and listening as they fly from perch to perch.

These owls can nest in a wide variety of sites, including stick nests of raptors, tree cavities, deserted buildings, and nest platforms. In the shrub-steppe of eastern Washington, I have seen Great Horned Owls nest in cliff-side cavities fifty feet above a river, where they have effective shelter from predators and the elements.

For owls smaller or more vulnerable than the Great Horned,

With a body that is small and light relative to its wing size, the Short-eared Owl can maneuver quickly and silently in flight.

After a day of roosting in the grass of Washington's Skagit River Delta, a Short-eared Owl shakes its body vigorously prior to taking flight.

cavity nesting is generally the rule. But where can one find reliable cavities in the drier open country of the interior West and Great Plains? Moist tall-grass areas give way to steppe covered with shorter grass, scrubland, and semidesert dry lands. Without sufficient moisture for grasses tall enough to hide a brooding female, let alone for shelter-providing trees, the burrows of rodents and other mammals are one of the only options.

And so it is that burrows, such as those created by prairie dogs, ground squirrels, badgers, marmots, skunks, armadillos,

kangaroo rats, and even tortoises, provide nest sites for the eponymous **Burrowing Owls**. If burrows are absent, these owls can excavate their own. An important characteristic of these burrows seems to be an entrance tunnel with a cavity significant enough to provide a dark nest chamber. The nest chamber itself is usually quite spherical. These semicolonial nesters seem to prefer burrows with close proximity to other adequate burrows. They often use the same burrow year after year.

Burrowing Owls traditionally have inhabited much of the

dry landscape of North America from the southern Canadian prairies through much of the Great Plains and western interior to central California and south to Mexico. (An isolated subspecies occurs in Florida.) They prefer burrows surrounded by short grass, with taller grass for foraging not far away. These areas are often treeless, but the presence of a tall shrub, fence post, or rail appears to be a habitat requirement, allowing the owls to spot approaching trouble. Much of this type of land has been converted to agriculture and recreation, so habitat in many areas is limited to the edges of undercultivated lands, grazing areas, ball fields, and airports. Prairie dog towns historically provided ideal habitat, where a pair or several pairs, forming a loose colony, might

nest. The Zuni Indians of the American Southwest observed this common association and called the Burrowing Owl the "priest of the prairie dogs" and believed that it lived in peace with prairie dogs, rattlesnakes, and horned lizards.

Lizards and young prairie dogs, however, are among the prey of Burrowing Owls. Lacking both superior nocturnal eyesight and exceptional hearing, they are opportunistic hunters, with daytime captures of small invertebrates such as beetles, crickets, locusts, earwigs, and scorpions providing the majority of their food during spring and summer and nighttime captures of rodents contributing the majority of sustenance during winter. These owls pursue their prey by running after it on the ground,

River deltas like this one in British Columbia often feature wet grass areas favored by rodents, wintering Short-eared Owls and, occasionally, irruptive Snowy Owls.

flying to it, pouncing on it from a perch, and even catching it on the wing. Usually prey is captured with the feet and transferred to the bill before being delivered to the young.

Knowing that Burrowing Owls are active at twilight, I was trying to get to the scrublands of the Columbia Plateau of central Washington before the sun set. I arrived to a purple-black evening, and several of them were waiting for me like guards of the grasslands: four small, flat-headed, long-legged, gargoyle-like owls capping consecutive fence posts. This common greeting stance inspired early pioneers to nickname them "Howdy Owls."

During my observations in central Washington and northern California, I saw Burrowing Owls constantly on alert for predators while appearing to be unconcerned by my presence. They paid particular attention to noises originating from the air and to shadows, whether of a crow or an airplane, and rotated their heads skyward in response to threatening sounds or shadows. The quick dash of one bird could initiate a colonywide bolt into their burrows. At other times, if a dog wandered by, the owls would bob their heads and screech, initiating another retreat. Various raptors, domestic dogs and cats, badgers, weasels, and skunks prey upon them.

Burrowing Owls carefully line their tunnel entrances and nest chambers with animal feces to disguise their own scent. Experiments have shown that when feces are removed from the entrance tunnel, the owls replace them within one day. They use feces from previous occupants, as well as cows, horses, and even dogs. It is possible that these linings also provide insulation and help keep the nest dry.

Most of the northern populations are migratory, moving south and west for winter. Nonmigratory birds retain pair bonds, while those returning for spring will choose a new mate every year. Males arrive on the breeding territory either singly or paired and then occupy and prepare a burrow while initiating territorial behaviors. Burrow preparation and maintenance involve digging with their bills and kicking soil backward with their feet. Burrowing Owls appears to be territorial only in relation to the burrow itself, while multiple individuals will share hunting areas. The primary call heard at this time of year is described as *coo coooo.*

Two Short-eared Owls demonstrate their moth-like bouncing flight as they confront each other in a territorial squabble.

Females typically lay their first eggs within a few weeks of arriving. When they have plenty of food, they generally produce more and larger eggs. Once the chicks hatch, they respond to disturbances at the nest by buzzing like rattlesnakes to deter potential predators. In areas where prey is reduced by poison or other means, brood success rates are low. Weather can play a role in nest failure as well. Burrows in soft ground are vulnerable

Opposite: Long-eared Owls leave their hidden daytime roosts to hunt as night falls.

to collapse during heavy rains, and such events can trap and drown nestlings and adults.

Burrowing Owls are in trouble throughout much of their range, with populations declining by 48 percent over the past forty years. The mowing of some fields and the draining of others have helped increase the range of Burrowing Owl populations in some areas, particularly Florida, where residential and industrial locations support the highest densities.

Unfortunately, human activities are causing more harm than benefit. The intensive cultivation of prairies and grasslands has been the greatest cause of the decline of this species. Cultivation removes burrows, which provide nesting and roosting habitat; it also removes native grass areas necessary for foraging. Destruction of prairie dog towns and plowing to remove badger and other mammal burrows destroy potential nest sites. Other pest-control efforts, such as use of insecticides and strychnine-coated grain

After consuming the head of its prey, a Burrowing Owl looks skyward for predators.

Similar in size to the Short-eared Owl, the northern harrier hawk can be distinguished by its more parallel wing position in flight and less noticeable wing flapping, as well as by its longer tail.

to control ground squirrels, likely contribute to population declines. Ironically, Burrowing Owl colonies do a good job of reducing populations of some of the very insects and small mammals that are being targeted with chemicals and other control measures. Illegal shooting for sport also takes its toll on Burrowing Owl populations.

Captive breeding programs, artificial burrows, grassland conservation and restoration efforts, and partnerships with landowners offer hope for protecting populations. Working in their favor is the tendency of these bold owls to accept human presence and observation, endearing them to the people they rely upon for their conservation.

6

Southwestern Dry Lands

The dry habitats of the Southwest range from southeastern California through south Texas. All these areas share the distinction of hosting several species of woodpeckers and owls otherwise found only in Mexico.

The Sonoran Desert lies south of the shrub-steppe and grasslands of the interior West in extreme southeastern California, southern Arizona, and northwestern Mexico. With rocky soils and less than five inches of rain annually, neither grass nor abundant burrows are possible; instead, ironwood, mesquite, palo verde, and saguaro cactus stud the landscape. The saguaros grow in valleys and drainage channels, where they soak up what little moisture is available.

The spiked arms of thirty-foot-tall saguaros were silhouetted by the purple-dawn May sky. It was 5:15 AM, fifteen minutes before sunrise in the Sonoran Desert near Tucson, and I was hoping to photograph owls returning to day roosts. A dark shape bounced in flight through the dawn from the top of one cactus to another. To my surprise, it was a woodpecker, not an owl. Moving in quietly, I watched as the yellow pollen-painted face of a **Gila Woodpecker** peered at me over the lip of a creamy-white saguaro flower.

A saguaro produces up to 200 flowers that bloom over a month or so, with a few opening each night and secreting nectar into their tubes to lure pollinators; they close before noon, never to open again. During these few weeks Gila Woodpeckers, as well as **Gilded Flickers**, begin their rounds before sunrise, taking advantage of the small nectar window, and in doing so play a major role in the pollination of this important plant.

The Gila is a medium-size woodpecker closely related to the Red-bellied and Golden-fronted Woodpeckers. Like them, it has a heavily barred back and mostly tan body. Males are distinguished from females by their red crown and larger size. The Gila is noisy, with several harsh calls, such as a single-frequency *kirrr* and a slow *kih-wrr ki-wrr*.

Although the Gila is usually associated with saguaros, it can also be found in riparian woodlands and residential areas with native trees or cacti sufficiently large for nest cavities. This nonmigratory bird lives primarily in southern Arizona but also in slivers of southern Nevada, southeastern California, southwestern New Mexico, and into Mexico. It is found from sea level to about 3,300 feet.

From May to July, Gila Woodpeckers focus their feeding efforts on the flowers and fruit of saguaro and other cacti, and in the process pollinate and spread seeds, which pass undamaged through their digestive tracts. During November and December, they concentrate on the berries of mistletoe. At other times, Gilas

Opposite: A male Gila Woodpecker feeds upon nectar of the saguaro's flowers.

Ferruginous Pygmy-Owl chicks await their return to the nest box after being banded and weighed as part of a long-term research project.

consume mostly insects. Ants, grasshoppers, cicadas, termites, moths, butterflies, and insect larvae are commonly chosen. Lizards and bird eggs are reportedly also part of the diet.

Saguaro cacti do not develop cavities naturally. Gila Woodpeckers and Gilded Flickers play a vital role in creating cavities for over thirty species of birds that nest in saguaros, including Elf Owls, Ferruginous Pygmy-Owls, Western Screech-Owls, ash-throated flycatchers, brown-crested flycatchers, cactus wrens, Lucy's warblers, great crested flycatchers, purple martins, and American kestrels. Woodpeckers excavate saguaros only during February in Arizona, then allow the cactus's soft inner pulp to heal and harden for several months before taking possession of the cavity. Timing is critical, as the woodpecker must move in after the cactus has hardened but before another cavity nester like the insidious European starling moves in.

North-facing tall cacti in flat, low-lying areas with a high saguaro density are the preferred nest sites. Gila Woodpecker nest height is related to the height of the cactus, with cavities

A male Golden-fronted Woodpecker with a grasshopper for his young

created in thick parts of the saguaro as low as three feet or as high as twenty-three feet. They tend to be excavated lower in taller cacti and are used for several consecutive years. The cavities are naturally preserved as the saguaros grow, contributing to the wider vertical distribution of their cavities. In contrast, Gilded Flicker nests have much less variability, always being excavated near the top of the saguaro, sometimes to the detriment or death of the cactus.

Breeding for Gilas begins in April with the young from the first clutch raised from May through June. Second clutches are common, with eggs laid in July and young fledglings appearing in September.

Populations of Gila Woodpeckers have declined in southeastern California over the past few decades. The greatest threats to the Gila Woodpecker are human development of the Sonoran Desert and nest-cavity competition from European starlings. These woodpeckers can live in suburban and urban environments provided that native vegetation, particularly the saguaro cactus, remains.

The Gilded Flicker occupies a range and habitat almost identical to those of the Gila Woodpecker, and its populations have also experienced declines for similar reasons, except that it does not seem to suffer from competition with starlings.

Larger and stronger than the Gila Woodpecker, the Gilded Flicker is virtually identical to the Northern Flicker and was only recently recognized as a separate species. Although its calls, food preferences, and ground foraging are the same as those of its northern relative, it is slightly smaller, with slight plumage differences. Unlike either subspecies of Northern Flicker, the Gilded possesses a cinnamon-colored forehead that transitions to an all-brown crown and nape. Other physical features mix those of the Red-shafted and Yellow-shafted subspecies, as it sports yellow underwings like the Yellow-shafted and a red mustache like the Red-shafted.

Many of the secondary cavity nesters that normally rely on the cavities provided by the Gila Woodpecker and Gilded Flicker also live in the dry brushlands and open woodlands of south Texas, where neither of these woodpeckers is found. In such areas, a close relative of the Gila Woodpecker, the **Golden-fronted Woodpecker**, fills the role of creating cavities.

The Golden-fronted is so closely related to the Gila and the Red-bellied Woodpeckers that it hybridizes with both where ranges overlap. If you took the Gila Woodpecker, added an orange-yellow nape patch, and increased its length by half an inch, you would have a hard time distinguishing it from the Golden-fronted Woodpecker. Even the vocalizations of the two woodpeckers are similar, although the Golden-fronted Woodpecker's call is much louder and harsher. The louder Golden-fronted drums a bit more than the Gila, especially during breeding season, when a few taps are followed by a series of rolling drums.

Like other members of the *Melanerpes* genus of woodpeckers, the Golden-fronted is omnivorous, eating fruits and nuts as much as insects, and is also unlikely to excavate deeply; instead, it probes and catches insects on the fly.

Highly adaptable, this woodpecker lives in relatively open woodlands and brushlands, including urban and suburban areas. As a result, both its population and range are expanding northward and westward, where it excavates in trees, utility poles, and fence posts and even utilizes nest boxes. This is one woodpecker not shy about reusing a cavity.

The Gila Woodpecker, Gilded Flicker, and Golden-fronted Woodpecker play keystone roles in the dry ecosystems from southeastern California to southern Texas. Among several cavity nesters that rely upon them is a rare species, the **Ferruginous Pygmy-Owl**, which lives in the Sonoran Desert scrub and adjacent semidesert grasslands in Arizona and in the mesquite brush and live oak woodlands of south Texas.

Thousands of stars brightened the inky-black sky when I was lucky enough to first see a Ferruginous. A researcher and I hiked through semidesert grassland habitat in the Altar Valley of south-central Arizona. Stooping low to traverse a prickly mesquite thicket, we crossed a dry, sandy streambed and weaved through thorny vegetation on the other side. On a rise above this drainage, an old saguaro stretched two arms tattooed with cavities skyward. This cactus hosted a family of Gilded Flickers and a family of Ferruginous Pygmy-Owls. Arriving before sunrise, my objective was to photograph the Ferruginous hunting during the early morning hours, one of this owl's two peak hunting periods. The Flicker came first, bouncing through the darkness to bury its bill in a milky-white saguaro bloom. Moments later, in a flash of feathers, a

Next page: As this Gilded Flicker moves between blossoms, he serves a valuable role in the pollination of saguaros.

Ferruginous Pygmy-Owl barreled into view and slammed against the Flicker, which squawked and flew off.

The Ferruginous Pygmy-Owl, like its close relative the Northern Pygmy-Owl, is a small, aggressive, long-tailed raptor with false eyes on the back of its head. The word *ferruginous* means "resembling iron rust in color" and describes its more reddish brown color compared to the darker brown of the

A Texas spiny lizard will be the next meal for the young of this Ferruginous Pygmy-Owl.

northern species, with tail bars also ferruginous rather than white. The streaked crown of the Ferruginous also distinguishes it from the Northern Pygmy-Owl, which has a spotted crown.

Both of these owls use a variety of vocalizations, depending upon the situation, but the primary call used by males is perhaps the easiest way to differentiate between the two. The male advertising call in both species can be described as *toots,* but the Northern Pygmy-Owl's is typically one or two hollow *toots* with a second or two between them, while the Ferruginous Pygmy-Owl's is a series of a few to a hundred evenly spaced notes prior to a pause. These notes are made at a higher pitch and with a faster delivery than those of the Northern Pygmy-Owl.

The ranges of these two owls overlap in Arizona, but the Northern Pygmy-Owl lives at much higher elevations, where it nests exclusively in tree cavities, while cacti are used most often by the Ferruginous Pygmy-Owl. Two subspecies of Ferruginous inhabit arid landscapes in the southernmost parts of the United States. The Cactus Ferruginous Pygmy-Owl, as the Arizona subspecies is often called, is a rare resident of the Sonoran Desert scrub and semidesert grasslands between 1,000 and 4,000 feet in elevation in south-central Arizona, although dispersing young are known to cross mountain passes rising more than 5,000 feet. Its natural environment overlaps with that of the Gila Woodpecker and Gilded Flickers, but this species prefers edges and openings of various sizes between patches of vegetation, particularly riparian areas and dry washes. The Texas subspecies, sometimes called the Ridgway's Ferruginous Pygmy-Owl, breeds in live oak-honey mesquite woodlands, mesquite brush, and riparian areas in south Texas.

The Ferruginous Pygmy-Owl relies upon woodpecker cavities for nesting, cover, and food caching. In Arizona, it nests mainly in saguaro cavities created by Gila Woodpeckers and Gilded Flickers and, rarely, in tree cavities thought to be excavated by Ladder-backed Woodpeckers. In Texas, its cavities are often formed by Golden-fronted Woodpeckers, although it also uses natural cavities and nest boxes. When given a choice between the larger Gilded Flicker and smaller Gila Woodpecker cavities, some evidence suggests it will select the smaller Gila cavity, probably an advantage against predation. This owl also prefers nest locations with greater understory cover nearby.

The number of available cavities may be one factor in determining which territories are chosen and defended, as the additional cavities might be enlisted for secondary nest sites if the first is predated, as occasional roosts for the male, and for caching food. When breeding season begins, males establish territories and call in females that inspect each cavity several times before selecting one in which to nest.

Nestlings of woodpeckers are potential prey for this opportunistic hunter, which hunts from perches or flies into cavities to look for food. In Arizona, reptiles, especially lizards, represent the largest percentage of its diet because they are quite abundant in the same habitat and tend to be active at the same time as the owls. Birds are more difficult to catch and thus are taken less often. The remainder of the diet is made up of small mammals and, less frequently, insects. The relative abundance of prey shifts seasonally, as colder temperatures in winter months reduce the availability of both reptiles and insects.

Ferruginous Pygmy-Owls are considered common in many areas of Mexico, Central America, and South America, but although taken off Texas's "threatened" list and Arizona's "endangered" list, nobody is certain how many of them exist in Texas, and Arizona populations are still considered unstable. Once common in dry riparian habitat in both areas, populations have fallen, particularly in Arizona, where the one survey taken since 1997 found no more than thirty-eight of these owls. Although these numbers are likely understated, as they do not reflect Ferruginous Pygmies that probably live in appropriate habitat on Tohono O'odham Indian Nation and other private lands, many previously occupied territories are now vacant, and this declining trend is likely the case throughout southern Arizona. In 2007, only six breeding pairs of Ferruginous Pygmy-Owls were found by Arizona Game and Fish researchers during nest-site monitoring.

All animals that live at the edge of their geographic range are sensitive to environmental change. And for populations of Ferruginous Pygmy-Owls in North America, the changes have been dramatic. Riparian habitat has been altered by several factors associated with development, including livestock grazing, conversion of land to agriculture, and the damming, piping, and diverting of streams and rivers. In Arizona, 85 percent of riparian habitat has been lost, and in the prime lower Rio Grande Valley habitat in Texas, 90 percent has been lost. In northern Mexico, the clearing of habitat for agriculture has been the primary culprit. The remaining fragmented populations in both Texas and Arizona are isolated from northern Mexican populations.

The brown-crested flycatcher is one of several secondary cavity nesters that utilize cavities created by the Gilded Flicker and Gila Woodpecker.

Pygmy-Owls are not migratory, and when they fly in the open they make low, short, point-to-point flights. Because of this, fragmentation of habitat by development of urban areas impairs the dispersal of young into new territories and the recruitment of unrelated mates from other areas. Urban areas also present hazards such as automobiles and increased numbers of natural and domestic predators that can further challenge populations. Impermeable border fences proposed for the United States-Mexico border would make the advantageous genetic mixing of Mexican populations of this low-flying bird and many other wildlife species even more difficult.

In Texas, much of the hope for this owl's survival lies with private landowners. Several of the most robust populations are nesting on large private ranches, and landowners have benefited from protection of habitat and nesting sites by charging birders and photographers for access. Fortunately, this species is able to live in proximity to humans, provided that natural or human-made cavities and proper habitat for hunting, nesting, and roosting are available. On some ranches, the habitat is actually improving.

Working to supplement Arizona populations, the Arizona Game and Fish Department, in coordination with the U.S. Fish & Wildlife Service, is conducting feasibility studies to determine if supplementing Arizona populations with captive-bred Ferruginous Pygmy-Owls is possible. So far, however, none of the eggs laid in captivity have been viable.

Southeast Arizona is a great place to see the life zone concept in play. The Sonoran Desert near Tucson sits at 2,300 feet. At higher elevations, desert transitions into grasslands before eventually becoming the foothills of the Sierra Madre Occidental Range of Mexico. The northernmost fingers of this range reaching into the United States include the Atascosa, Santa Rita, Huachuca, and Chiricahua Mountains. At around 4,500 feet, Madrean pine-oak woodlands blanket the slopes and contain species of birds found nowhere else in the United States, including the Arizona Woodpecker and the Whiskered Screech-Owl. At progressively higher elevations within these southern mountains, the forest transitions between communities very familiar farther north; stands of ponderosa pine are followed by Douglas-fir and aspen, finally giving way to stands of Engelmann spruce. These mountain ranges are surrounded by desert scrub and are collectively referred to as the Sky Islands.

Dusk was imminent as I stood in a backyard on the eastern foothills of the Huachuca Mountains. Several impossibly plump Acorn Woodpeckers chattered and flew back and forth noisily from a cavity-pocked telephone pole to neighboring trees. It was hard to imagine that any owl, much less the world's smallest, would want to nest close to such a raucous bunch. Yet immediately after the last Acorn Woodpecker retreated to its cavity and dusk dropped its dark screen, a soft whistle-like *peeu* came from the adjacent cavity in the telephone pole as the tiny, fluffy, golden-eyed face of an **Elf Owl** popped out. From the shrubs behind, a high-pitched puppylike yelping began: *peeu* followed by a rapid, descending *pe, pe, pe, pe, pe, pe.* Darting from the cavity, the owl flew into the shrubs nearby. For the next several hours I stood in the dark among the thorny shrubs, listening, before turning on my flashlight, for the faint sound of an owl's talons clicking against a branch or brushing against a leaf as it landed. The light did not disturb them, and each beam of light revealed new vignettes of their hunt: the owl scanning below before diving down to hover over the ground; the owl looking directly at me as it rested on a branch; the owl transferring a Jerusalem cricket from its talons to its bill before departing.

With its cryptic brown plumage and retiring habits, the Arizona Woodpecker is very difficult to locate outside of breeding season.

After capturing a Jerusalem cricket with his talons, an Elf Owl carries it in his mouth in order to bring it back to his offspring.

A nimble female Ladder-backed Woodpecker tastes the sweet nectar of the ocotillo.

North American Elf Owls are migratory, spending their winters in southern Mexico and breeding in three populations along the U.S.–Mexico border from river valleys and desert washes to 6,000 feet up in mountain canyons. Although common in the saguaro cacti of the Sonoran Desert, Elf Owl populations reach higher densities in the cooler mid-elevation (4,500–5,250 feet) Madrean pine-oak woodlands of the Sky Islands. Stable populations are also found in northwestern New Mexico and in the desert scrub, riverside cottonwoods, and sycamores of southern and western Texas. Evidence suggests a preference for upland habitats if Ferruginous Pygmy-Owls are occupying the riparian areas of the region. In the absence of competition, Elf Owls nest in riparian woodlands along the Colorado River of southeastern California and southwestern Arizona; it is interesting that these owls can survive almost indefinitely in habitats that lack surface water.

Strictly nocturnal, the Elf Owl flies from twig to branch to flower top, waiting and watching for a moth, beetle, cricket, or one of the many other insects that make up most of its diet. When it spots prey, it flies low and directly and sometimes will hover before snatching the prey with its feet or bill. This owl also chases insects on foot and hangs from vegetation to probe flowers for insects attracted to nectar. It sometimes catches other prey, such as scorpions, snakes, lizards, and mice, and even caches them in its nest. Captured food is manipulated by moving it between the bill and feet to remove unwanted items like the dangerous stinger of a scorpion or the wings of a sphinx moth. The adults consume mostly insects, but spiders and scorpions are a large component of what they feed their young. Elf Owls are not silent fliers, which is probably not to their detriment considering their mostly invertebrate prey are believed to be less sensitive to noise.

Insects and reptiles benefit Elf Owls in ways other than as

The drylands of the Southwest and Texas, such as this part of the Sonoran Desert, feature owls and woodpeckers found nowhere else north of Mexico.

a food source. Occasionally, blind snakes are captured and delivered to the nest as food, only to escape and live in nest debris where they eat ant brood and fly maggots that might otherwise compete with nestlings for cached food. Tree ants often nest in Elf Owl cavities, and while they do not bother the owls, they will attack intruders.

Elf Owls nest in cavities created by woodpeckers, primarily the Gila Woodpecker and Gilded Flicker in the Sonoran Desert, Acorn and Arizona Woodpeckers in pine-oak woodlands, and Ladder-backed and Golden-fronted Woodpeckers in Texas. These owls also adapt to suburbia and will use woodpecker holes in telephone poles and even nest boxes when natural cavities are in short supply.

Cavity exposure varies by habitat. In south-central Arizona, cavity orientation appears random, while nearby in the hotter climate of the Sonoran Desert nest cavities are oriented to the north or northwest to benefit from less direct sun. To provide prey delivery perches in the Sonoran, Elf Owls choose cavities in saguaros that have ocotillo or ironwood in front of them. In forests, they choose Arizona sycamores with open fronts that allow a flyway and early visual detection of predators in this more heavily vegetated environment. In Texas, Elf Owls often nest in cavities in agave flower stalks, cottonwood, and mesquite.

Elf Owls frequently nest in the same tree, cactus, or telephone pole as up to three other species of birds and within close proximity of up to sixteen. Sometimes they will usurp cavities from tenants, including ash-throated flycatchers, Gila Woodpeckers, and Acorn Woodpeckers; at other times, it is they who are forced out by Acorn Woodpeckers or Western Screech-Owls. While they will tolerate the presence of small birds, neighboring Elf Owls will assist a nesting pair in mobbing such potential predators as snakes, Great Horned Owls, or ringtails.

Like Screech-Owls, male Elf Owls defend more than one cavity but ignore intrusions between them, and as a result territories often overlap. The alternative cavities are less likely to be found by a predator, so they serve effectively as roost sites and as second nest sites if the first should fail. With overlapping territories and nests sometimes less than 30 feet apart, populations can be quite dense. Once they have established territories, these owls do not roam far, with a maximum foraging distance of approximately 200 feet.

Desert populations of Elf Owls lay a few more eggs than canyon populations. A remarkable 90 percent of all eggs result in fledged young, which is likely a result of the difficulty predators have accessing Elf Owl nests.

At its western range limit in southeastern California, the Elf Owl is a state endangered species due to habitat destruction. Elf Owl populations have probably declined overall in Arizona due to conversion of habitat in and around Tucson and Phoenix. In the Sonoran Desert, Elf Owls may still be the most common raptor, but only a quarter of the Sonoran habitat is adequately protected from conversion to other uses. Within this habitat, Elfs are most common where there is significant mesquite and perennial vegetation cover, as well as dense populations of saguaros.

From a conservation standpoint, there is reason for optimism, too, as these birds can adapt to suburbanized areas with native vegetation and will even use nest boxes. In the past, some populations have recolonized areas after local disappearance. Furthermore, populations in the Sky Islands and in Texas appear to be stable.

Elf Owls' calls announce the arrival of March in the Sonoran Desert, while a few weeks later in the higher Sky Islands these owls are an integral part of the most dense and diverse dusk chorus I have ever heard as their puppylike yelps mix with the bouncing-ball *hoots* of Western Screech-Owls and steady high whistles of Whiskered Screech-Owls.

Although the ranges of the Western Screech-Owl, Whiskered Screech-Owl, and Flammulated Owl overlap to some degree in southeastern Arizona, these three members of the *Otus* (Screech-Owl) genus occupy distinct habitat niches on the mountain slopes of the Sky Islands. The Western Screech-Owls occupy the lowest elevation from the desert scrub and grasslands up into the more open parts of the pine-oak woodland, where Whiskered Screech-Owls are also found. In the majority of the pine-oak woodland, the Whiskered Screech-Owl is the only member of the genus until the forest transitions again at higher elevations to the more open mixed coniferous forest, where Flammulated Owls appear. In the core of this zone, mountain conifers more commonly associated with northern latitudes, including ponderosa pine and Douglas-fir, are found in isolated stands and provide a hospitable habitat for the Flammulated.

The Sierra Madrean pine-oak woodland, however, is the only

A Whiskered Screech-Owl suns itself in a natural cavity in a sycamore tree.

A Ferruginous Pygmy-Owl pauses momentarily after delivering food to his young in a saguaro cactus.

region of North America where the **Whiskered Screech-Owl** is found. A very close relative of the Western Screech-Owl, the smaller Whiskered Screech-Owl is differentiated by a couple of minor physical features and by its call. The whiskers, or hairlike bristles on the ends of the feathers edging the facial disk and bill, give this owl its name but are difficult to see in the field. Its gold orange eyes, rusty feather tones, and small feet are the other commonly cited physical differences, but all seem very difficult to identify unless the two species are perched side by side. On the other hand, the evenly spaced call consisting of a group of several whistles is easily distinguished from the Western Screech-Owl's bouncing-ball call of accelerating short whistles.

Much of the life history of the Whiskered Screech-Owl is very similar to that of the Western Screech, except that insects are more important in its diet than rodents, given its smaller size. Surprisingly aggressive, this owl appears to be dominant over other owls it lives near, including the larger Western Screech-Owl. It nests in natural cavities in sycamore and oak trees, cavities excavated by Northern Flickers, or perhaps those excavated by smaller woodpeckers and later enlarged by squirrels.

Like the owl genus *Otus*, the Woodpecker genus *Picoides* also has three members in the Sky Islands, whose ranges cover a continuum of habitats from desert scrub to mixed coniferous forests. Hairy Woodpeckers are found at the highest elevations. The Arizona Woodpecker breeds at slightly lower elevations in the pine-oak woodlands, and the Ladder-backed Woodpecker occupies the arid landscapes from the grasslands to the desert scrub.

As with the Whiskered Screech-Owl, the only areas of North America in which the **Arizona Woodpecker** is found are the Sierra Madrean woodlands of southeastern Arizona and southwestern New Mexico. The Arizona Woodpecker is unlikely to be confused with any other woodpecker because it is the only woodpecker in North America with a solid brown back. A highly sought-after target for birders hoping to see Mexican species, this is a very difficult bird to find after mating season, as it becomes silent and reclusive once its eggs are laid. One Arizona Woodpecker has been witnessed aggressively chasing an Acorn Woodpecker away from its nest while remaining silent the entire time.

In southeast Arizona, this woodpecker forages in evergreen oaks, sycamores, and pines, where it feeds upon insects, fruits, and acorns. It often forages near the ground and then works its way up a tree before flying to the base of a nearby tree and repeating the pattern. Although it appears to be most closely related to the Hairy Woodpecker based upon vocalizations, plumage, and behavior, the Arizona spends the majority of its time flaking bark and probing rather than excavating the way the Hairy does. During winter, the Hairy and Arizona Woodpeckers both move downslope, where they sometimes share habitat with their lower-elevation relatives.

The **Ladder-backed Woodpecker** is a small, nimble woodpecker related to the Downy and the Nuttall's Woodpeckers and fills a niche in the arid Southwest very similar to the niche its relatives fill in other regions. In fact, the ranges of these three woodpeckers overlap only in a small area in California.

The Ladder-backed is slightly larger than the Downy but slightly smaller than its look-alike, the Nuttall's Woodpecker. The physical differences between the Ladder-backed and Nuttall's are minimal, primarily consisting of red markings on the male covering more of the head, white barring extending farther up the back, and a thinner black stripe behind the eye of the Ladder-backed. Even their calls and drumming are very similar.

This small, kinetic, unorthodox woodpecker searches for insects on low plants and small branches of trees, covering the surfaces untouched by other woodpeckers throughout the Southwest. It occurs throughout the low- to mid-elevation deserts, desert scrub, semidesert grasslands, and thorn forests of the Southwest and arid landscapes of south Texas, where it often forages upon and nests in cacti of various types. Although found in pine-oak woodlands in Central America and in pinyon-juniper in Colorado, the Ladder-backed prefers the most arid landscapes of North America.

And those arid landscapes, from southeastern California through southern Arizona to southern Texas, particularly lowland and riparian areas, have been drastically altered by development and agriculture. This alteration threatens several species, most notably the Ferruginous Pygmy-Owl, whose most stable refuges lie within protected parks and reserves in Arizona and on large ranches in south Texas. Fortunately, several of the birds of this arid region, including Gila Woodpeckers, Gilded Flickers, and Elf Owls, adapt well to human presence. Landscaping with and retaining native vegetation in residential areas can help retain linkages to otherwise fragmented habitat—to benefit all of these species uniquely adapted to the most arid landscapes.

7

Southeastern Pine Forests

Northeast Texas marks the beginning of the longleaf pine ecosystem, which stretches across the coastal plains of Louisiana, Alabama, Florida, Georgia, and the Carolinas. This system once covered 90 million acres; now roughly 3 million remain.

Lightning and the fires it ignites have shaped the longleaf pine ecosystem. Fires fueled by wiregrass and dry pine needles clear out woody vegetation that is not fire resistant and expose mineral-rich soil conducive to seed germination. The result is an open forest dominated by large older pines, with a well-developed ground layer of grasses and forbs and virtually no mid-story. This is the ideal habitat for the endangered **Red-cockaded Woodpecker**, the keystone species of this system.

The Red-cockaded Woodpecker is a small, mostly black-and-white woodpecker with a few usually hidden red feathers in the crown of the male. It occurs sporadically in mature open pine forests throughout the southeastern United States. Longleaf is the preferred species of pine, but it also uses loblolly, slash, short-leaf, Virginia, pond, and pitch. In all cases, properly maintained habitat requires fire every one to five years, which usually comes in summer as a result of lightning. Currently prescribed, or intentionally set, burns are ignited periodically to mimic historic fire frequencies, but in many areas this is becoming more difficult with increasing development of forested landscape.

Most other woodpeckers prefer to nest in soft deciduous trees, but frequent fires do not allow such trees to grow large enough for suitable cavities in the longleaf pine ecosystem. The Red-cockaded Woodpecker has adapted by becoming the only woodpecker to nest exclusively in live pine trees. Pine trees are notoriously hard, so a family group works together to excavate cavities in mature pine trees over eighty years old that are infested with red heart fungus. The excavation begins below the lowest living branch.

Even with fungal infestation, the excavation is slow because pine trees, particularly longleaf pines, produce prodigious amounts of sap. More than one Red-cockaded Woodpecker has been found dead after being trapped by the sticky substance; to avoid this fate, these birds must take long breaks to allow the sap to harden during excavations of the sapwood until they reach the decayed heartwood.

Each Red-cockaded Woodpecker requires its own cavity to roost in at night, with cavity-containing trees tending to be clustered together. These tree clusters house members of a family group, as well as some nonbreeding nonhelpers that forage with the group. The process of creating a cavity takes from one to twelve years. Once created, cavities are often reused, and they are known to have been used for as many as thirty consecutive years.

Opposite: The Red-cockaded Woodpecker is named for the few rarely visible red feathers on the side of the male's head.

A young Red-cockaded Woodpecker peers from a cavity surrounded by dried white sap.

Southeastern longleaf pine forests are characterized by widely spaced mature pines with a grass understory.

Each evening, the family group works together to create and maintain resin wells around the cavities. These wells ooze sap, which flows around and below the cavity, forming an effective barrier to most predators that might be tempted to raid the nest and making much of the trunk below the cavity appear white and candlelike.

Nest failure is rare for this species, but when it does occur it is usually due to predation, with climbing rat snakes being the main culprits. Southern flying squirrels are also a major threat, as they will eat eggs and small nestlings. Red-bellied and Red-headed Woodpeckers will do the same, albeit infrequently.

Red-cockaded cavities that get enlarged by other woodpeckers are then often abandoned by the Red-cockadeds, likely due to the predation opportunity larger cavities provide to Eastern Screech-Owls and American kestrels.

This is a cooperative-breeding species, with family groups consisting of one breeding male, one breeding female, and up to four helpers that are usually male offspring of the breeding pair. The breeding male's roosting cavity becomes the nest cavity for the family group. It is usually the most recently excavated and thus has the greatest sap flow of the cavities in the cluster.

Pairs are monogamous and often mate for life. Parents

The American kestrel is an obligate cavity nester that often uses the abandoned cavities of Red-cockaded Woodpeckers that have since been enlarged by Pileated Woodpeckers or Northern Flickers.

incubate most of the eggs, although the helpers do some of the work. Male helpers take more of a role in the brooding of chicks but let the parents do the majority of the feeding and nest sanitation work. Males are dominant in this highly structured community, and sometimes a first-year male may usurp a roost cavity from the breeding female.

Within each brood, most females leave to look for a female vacancy in another group while males usually remain as helpers.

Unlike the Acorn Woodpecker, if a male vacancy occurs, one of the nonbreeding male helpers will inherit his father's cavity and role and the breeding female will leave to look for a new opportunity. While a male may wait five years or more to inherit this position, the survival rate for birds that leave is much lower than for those that stay. Family groups with helpers successfully fledge many more birds than those without.

When not at the nest, family groups often forage together,

Opposite: A juvenile Red-headed Woodpecker can be distinguished from an adult by its brown head.

often in mixed flocks of birds of several species, including pine warblers, brown-headed nuthatches, and other woodpeckers, particularly in winter. Favored food includes insects, spiders, and centipedes, as well as other arthropods and their eggs and larvae, and a small amount of seeds and fruits. Males forage on branches and the higher trunks of pines, in contrast to females, which focus on sections of the trunk that are below the lowest branches. Almost 90 percent of foraging takes place on the largest pines that have the largest foraging surface. The primary foraging method involves the "scaling" of bark, which involves pecking bark plates from trees to reveal hidden prey. When bark has been scaled recently, the tree takes on a redder tone, a sure sign of a foraging territory. Throughout foraging, as with much of its behavior, this social species is constantly chattering with its buzzing *shirrit*.

Clearly, Red-cockaded Woodpeckers have a tremendous impact upon the longleaf pine, and other mature southeast pine, ecosystems. In these ecosystems, dead and soft-barked trees are rare, so the role of primary cavity creator falls upon this woodpecker. At least twenty-seven species of vertebrates will use its cavities, including Eastern Screech-Owls, eastern bluebirds, American kestrels, fox squirrels, insects, and bats. Other woodpeckers, including Red-bellied, Red-headed, and Pileated, will use and in some cases enlarge its cavities. The demise of this bird would result in the elimination and reduction of habitat for a whole host of other animals.

Due to the loss of 97 percent of the native longleaf pine habitat, Red-cockaded Woodpecker populations have dropped to 1 percent of historical numbers. In 1970 the bird was listed as "endangered"; with the passage of the Endangered Species Act in 1973, the remaining 10,000 birds received protection. Since then populations have risen to more than 15,000 birds in more than 6,000 family groups.

The remaining habitat and thus the remaining populations are fragmented, which creates big challenges for this nonmigratory bird. Old management plans categorized habitat quality by the number of trees rather than the size, ignoring the additional foraging surface provided by larger trees. Since this species tends to breed to its environment's maximum capacity, birds must move to new areas to increase their populations. Unfortunately,

the development of new groups and cavity clusters is rare for several reasons, including the time required for cavity construction, limited access to suitable trees for cavity excavation in the remaining fragmented habitat, inadequate foraging trees, and insufficient females to replace breeding females.

Approximately two-thirds of Red-cockaded Woodpecker populations are on federal lands, including national forests, national wildlife refuges, and military installations; the management of this habitat will likely determine the bird's fate. Measures being taken for the recovery of the species include prescribed burns, using cavity restrictors to prevent the enlargement of cavities by larger woodpeckers that would render cavities unsuitable, installing artificial cavities to enhance tree clusters and help establish new groups, and relocating juveniles to establish or stabilize a cluster.

When large trees in the longleaf pine zone die or are isolated at the edge of a forest, suitable cavity sites are lost for Red-cockaded Woodpeckers but become well suited for the **Red-headed Woodpecker**.

Woodpecker cavities can be challenging for people to find. For most species, nest trees usually look much like the others in an area. The nest trees of Red-headed Woodpeckers are often an exception. In my travels throughout Texas, Florida, and North Carolina, no matter the species of tree chosen, they looked the same: tall, dead, thick, sun-bleached, barkless, and standing alone or in a small clump with a medium-size round cavity or series of cavities near the top. Apparently the slick, barkless surface of these trees offers Red-headed Woodpeckers a defense from predators such as snakes. Red-headeds use the same tree, and often the same cavity, in consecutive years, although they also use cavities created by Red-cockaded Woodpeckers and Flickers. They occasionally use nest boxes.

Red-headed Woodpeckers are distinctive, medium-size woodpeckers. Males and females are the same size, and cannot be distinguished in the field, although juveniles are easily distinguished from adults by their brown heads. Throughout North American history, these birds have been given various nicknames, including "white-shirt," "half-a-shirt," "jellycoat," and "flag bird" due to their bright red heads and distinctly contrasting blocks of black-and-white plumage. They were also a

Opposite: The Red-headed Woodpecker often winters where nuts or other crops are available.

Brown-headed nuthatches often travel in mixed flocks with Red-cockaded Woodpeckers and feed upon the insects and grubs uncovered by the woodpeckers' bark scaling.

war symbol to the Cherokee, and Plains tribes used their heads as battle ornaments.

The Red-headed Woodpecker prefers forest openings and edges. Its fluctuating populations and changing distribution are determined by the availability of appropriate snags and abundance of food. It is found east of the Rocky Mountains in the United States and parts of southern Canada but is absent from northern and eastern New England, southern Florida, and the Appalachians.

Throughout its range, large old trees killed by disease, burns, or the flooding associated with beaver dams often lure nesting Red-headed Woodpeckers and can result in population spikes; conversely, the cutting of dead trees or dead limbs can eliminate local populations. In many areas with old, dead trees, the Red-headed Woodpecker is a keystone species, particularly in pine and oak habitats.

Two historical population peaks occurred in the mid-twentieth century in response to the death of chestnut trees from fungal chestnut blight and to the demise of American elms due to Dutch elm disease. Breeding and wintering populations of Red-headed Woodpeckers exploded exponentially across the Midwest following the demise of the elms and preceding the cutting of dead trees that then eliminated local populations.

The Red-headed Woodpecker is North America's most omnivorous woodpecker, consuming seeds and nuts, berries and other fruits, crops such as corn, insects, bird eggs and nestlings, mice, and even an occasional adult bird. It has a shorter tongue than other woodpeckers, and the barbs normally found at the tip of woodpeckers' tongues are replaced by hairlike structures, an adaptation to a more general diet.

Like Lewis's Woodpeckers, Red-headeds are experts at pursuing insects on the wing, a useful skill for birds of open woodlands. During the breeding season, they often spend half their time catching insects on the wing; another third of their time is spent pursuing prey on the ground—a rare practice for woodpeckers. Insect outbreaks draw Red-headed Woodpeckers in great numbers. Rocky Mountain locusts were a significant food source before their extinction, and today these birds congregate to feed upon cicadas and midges. Fruits of hardwood trees, such as acorns, beechnuts, and pecans, are the primary winter food, although if numbers are low, corn or other crops can be substituted. The birds' shifting winter range is defined by the availability of foods, as they move on once food supplies are exhausted.

The Red-headed is one of four woodpeckers in the world that commonly store food, but it is the only one known to hide its stored food by covering it with bark or wood. Like the Lewis's Woodpecker, it breaks nuts before storing them. Occasionally, insects such as grasshoppers are stored in a crevice in such a way that the insect is kept alive, legs waving in the air, until it is consumed.

While not territorial over the source of food, the Red-headed is the most pugnacious woodpecker. It is very aggressive toward other birds, especially other woodpeckers, near its food stores or nest trees. The Red-bellied Woodpecker shares much of the same habitat and food preferences as the Red-headed, resulting in frequent conflicts. The Red-headed Woodpecker is always dominant in these encounters and forces the Red-bellied into less optimal winter habitats. Even the much larger Flickers and Pileateds will defer to this aggressive bird.

Red-headed Woodpecker populations declined by approximately 63 percent between 1966 and 2005. Although they are adaptable to suburban and even some urban environments, their numbers in those areas have declined due to the removal of dead trees and branches. Once common throughout New England, they now can only be found in its westernmost parts. In rural areas, firewood cutting, clear-cutting, agricultural development, and the channeling of rivers are taking a toll on nesting habitat. Alas, much of the reforestation in the eastern United States, combined with fewer orchards, fewer chestnuts, the loss of oak-savanna habitat, fire suppression, and modern farming practices are all making habitat less than ideal. On a more positive note, the planting of trees in areas that were formerly prairie, particularly cottonwoods, which often develop dead branches and become snags, has resulted in local population increases and range expansions.

8

Eastern Suburban and Urban Habitats

Suburban and urban habitats in the East, like those in the West, serve as potential extensions or connections to surrounding native habitat. For owls and woodpeckers, the most important elements include properly located nesting places in the form of snags or nest boxes, species-specific food sources such as native plants and seeds, and a water source. Much of the best habitat exists, predictably, in large parks. With proper habitat, suburban and even some urban areas of eastern North America can host several interesting woodpeckers and owls, including the most important excavator in North America and the most colorful owl.

I was observing a **Yellow-shafted Flicker** cavity in the late spring in North Carolina. Two timid soft brown heads peered from the cavity as their parents cried *kwikwikwikwi* from a nearby tree in an attempt to lure the youngsters from the nest. Black mustaches identified both chicks as males. This appeared to be a small brood for this species. The parents flew to the nest tree as if to feed, then quickly departed and belted out another call from a distant tree. With a sudden burst of courage, one of the chicks gripped the lip of the cavity with its claws, thrust its head and breast out, and trustingly leapt from the cavity, its untested wings carrying it on a smooth, direct course to the waiting parents. Before I could back up and allow my fixed lens to capture the second fledgling, the more reluctant chick fol-

lowed the identical course. To my surprise, a third chick popped into the spot occupied by its predecessor, and after it fledged, a fourth bounced up and out of the cavity. This cavity appeared to be dispensing new Yellow-shafted Flickers like a Pez dispenser.

Yellow-shafted Flickers are the eastern subspecies of the Northern Flicker and can be distinguished from their western relatives by their black mustache, red nape crescent, and yellow feathers underneath their wings and tails. Being large and brown, they are unlikely to be confused with any other eastern or midwestern woodpecker; the undulating flight and distinctive white rump patch set apart all Northern Flickers from other woodpeckers while in flight.

The territorial displays of this common woodpecker often lend a golden edge to spring in midwestern and eastern North America. The yellow feathers under the wings and tail are not used to attract a mate but to display to birds of the same sex that infringe upon the territory of a mated pair. Often the mate will stand apart and watch the furious flagging and waving tail feathers of such encounters. Both sexes aggressively defend nesting territories against incursions from other flickers, although the size of the defended turf shrinks once incubation begins. These flickers seem unconcerned about the presence of other species, which sometimes nest in the same trees.

Opposite: A Yellow-shafted Northern Flicker is startled to find his mate poking her head from their cavity just as he arrives.

A mated pair of Eastern Screech-Owls display two color phases found in this species.

Like all flickers, the Yellow-shafted spends a lot of time on the ground in pursuit of ants in summer and beetle larvae in fall, but it is more likely to move to a diet of fruits in fall and winter than other flickers. This diet variation leads to a subtle shift in habitat, and this subspecies can often be found foraging for berries on trees in swamps and other places.

Northern Shafted Flickers (including both Red-shafted and Yellow-shafted) have declined 30 percent over the past forty years, probably as a result of removal of proper nesting places such as snags, dead limbs, and trees with heart rot, as well as competition for cavities from invasive European starlings. Still, the Yellow-shafted Flicker is found in all the eastern and midwestern states and provinces from Florida all the way to the edge of the tree line in Alaska. Like the Red-shafted Flicker, the Yellow-shafted is a habitat generalist but is best adapted to open woodlands regardless of tree species. It is often found at the edge of forests and meadows, a habitat common in suburban and rural parts of central and eastern North America. The Yellow-shafted Flicker adapts well to the presence of humans and can even be found nesting in large cities. Throughout most of its range, it serves as a keystone species due to its role as the most important cavity excavator, providing nest sites for dozens of species of birds, including eastern bluebirds, American kestrels, Northern Saw-whet Owls, and Eastern Screech-Owls.

When my friend Dan asked me to be his best man, he wasn't expecting me to throw him a wild bachelor party, but I'm not sure he expected to be out looking for owls two nights before his wedding, either. We were in southwestern Florida, a promising place to find the red phase of the **Eastern Screech-Owl**. Within fifteen minutes of initiating their call in a suburban park, owls were responding to me. A gray adult was the first to show its yellow eyes, but the bird's color was disappointingly similar to that of the Western Screech-Owls of the West Coast. Minutes later, a second owl flew in. Rich, reddish-brown plumage was illuminated by our flashlights. We excitedly snapped shots of our targeted bird, happy that our quest had been successful. Later, as we were heading back to get some rest before the wedding preparations, we called a final time, and to our astonishment a brightly colored orange-red owl confronted us and was quickly joined by her very dark gray mate, representing a range of colors far broader than we had imagined.

An Eastern Screech-Owl delivers a worm to a hungry youngster. (It should be noted that the viewing hole into this cavity was created years before these owls selected it. All the owlets in the pictured brood fledged successfully.)

The subtle reddish wash on the belly of the Red-bellied Woodpecker gives this species its name.

The tufted titmouse often builds its nest in an abandoned woodpecker cavity.

The Eastern Screech-Owl is a medium-size owl with the widest color range of any North American owl. Although the gray phases of the Eastern and Western Screech-Owls look very similar, the call, a soft trill (or whinny), clearly distinguishes this bird from its western relative. The striking red, or rufous, phase is found in more than a third of the birds rangewide, but in the middle elevations of its eastern range, between one-half and three-quarters are this color. In the western part of its range fewer than 15 percent are rufous; in many areas, such as southern Texas, all the Eastern Screech-Owls are gray. The genetically dominant rufous color morph offers advantages and disadvantages that influence its distribution. Rufous owls are more difficult to see in low light, at night, and under cloudy conditions, providing them a competitive advantage over gray morphs in more overcast areas.

On the other hand, because rufous feathers contain less of the pigment melanin than black or gray feathers, and because melanin increases feather durability, the feathers of rufous owls are less resilient to damage and wear than gray ones, leading to a competitive disadvantage in dry, dusty areas. Darker feathers also dry faster and are thought to offer greater insulation than rufous or other light-colored feathers, which may explain the

Two young male Yellow-shafted Northern Flickers prepare to leave the nest cavity as their parents call to them from a distance.

A young Eastern Screech-Owl peers from the nest cavity entrance.

In suburban parks, yards, vacant lots, and greenbelts, they can be housed by old shade and fruit trees with natural or flicker-created cavities for nesting. Greenbelts and riparian areas are necessary for populations to spread.

The Eastern Screech-Owl is the owl best adapted to urban and suburban habitats, and by most measures fares better in these environments than it does in rural areas. Several factors contribute to its success. Not only does it acclimate to human presence; it also finds a greater food supply, fewer predators, and a warmer environment in suburban habitat. Studies in both Texas and Connecticut have shown suburban populations to be between two and six times as dense as rural ones. Suburban populations appear to be more stable over time with a regular distribution, while rural populations are more cyclical and patchy. Several habitat factors seem to be associated with quality suburban habitat, including a constant source of water (particularly running water), wet woodlands, edge habitat, open unmowed areas, and cavities or nest boxes. As the proportion of evergreen softwood trees increases, Screech-owl populations decline, particularly in dry upland habitats. Eastern Screech-Owl populations are unlikely to dwindle due in large part to their ability to thrive in suburban habitats, which for this species appears to offset losses of habitat in more rural areas.

Not surprisingly given its range of habitats, the Eastern Screech-Owl is an opportunistic predator, taking a wide range of prey: insects, earthworms, small mammals (including rats, mice, shrews, moles, bats, chipmunks, and flying squirrels), various kinds of birds, crayfish, and even fish. Birds are a primary prey, a fact not lost on the parents of young birds that will mob Eastern Screech-Owls, not to scare them off but to teach naïve youngsters of the danger. The strong correlation between the birds that are most often preyed upon—including northern cardinals, chickadees, and white-throated sparrows—and the ones that most frequently mob this owl is not accidental.

Like the Eastern Screech-Owl, the **Red-bellied Woodpecker** has benefited from the presence of humans, expanding its range northward partly in response to the availability of backyard feeders and westward into the Great Plains by taking advantage of both the feeders and planted woodlands along river bottoms.

The Red-bellied Woodpecker is now found throughout much of the eastern United States and into southern Ontario. The ranges of Red-bellied and Golden-fronted Woodpeckers

higher survival rates of dark Eastern Screech-Owls during harsh winters and in cold climates.

Eastern Screech-Owls are year-round residents of most of the United States east of the Rocky Mountains and a small part of southeastern Saskatchewan and southern Manitoba. Throughout this range they take advantage of open woods below 4,500 feet with a preference for oaks, cottonwoods, and mesquites.

overlap in Texas, where these close relatives are highly aggressive toward each other.

Although the Red-bellied adapts to a variety of habitats, it prefers moist forests with larger trees, greater tree density, and greater midstory and understory density than those preferred by the Red-cockaded Woodpecker, Red-headed Woodpecker, and Northern Flicker. Nest cavities are usually created in large snags; in places where snags are not available, this woodpecker often nests in fence posts or utility poles.

Red-bellied Woodpeckers usually excavate their own cavities but are also known to pull Red-cockadeds from their nests, sometimes injuring or killing these endangered woodpeckers in the process. Surprisingly, they are able to use these usurped cavities without enlarging them. New nest cavities are normally excavated in a dead tree each year, often on the underside of a limb or leaning trunk, and often below the prior year's cavity. These cavities normally have bark around the entrance hole, unlike those of Red-headed Wodpeckers.

Red-bellieds are not shy about evicting smaller birds from food sources either and have been known to supplant Yellow-bellied Sapsuckers at their sap wells. Although also dominant over Red-cockaded and Golden-fronted Woodpeckers, they are submissive to Pileated and Red-headed Woodpeckers, with adults even giving a wide berth to juvenile Red-headeds. Their aggressive nature has allowed the Red-bellied Woodpecker to be one of the few woodpeckers that is able to retain its cavity against aggressive attempts by the usually dominant European starling.

Like the related Golden-fronted and Gila Woodpeckers, the Red-bellied is an omnivore, eating a wide variety of food from insects and mast (acorns and nuts) to fruit. The Red-bellied takes food flexibility even further by hunting baby birds (including Red-cockaded), lizards, and even frogs. This bird has a highly flexible cylindrical tongue that is both pointed and barbed, which enables it to better spear and pull prey from cracks and crevices.

As with Pacific Coast urban and suburban habitat, leaving dead wood, providing nest boxes, protecting and planting native plants, avoiding the use of pesticides, and attempting to mimic native habitat in backyards are the best ways to protect native populations. Fortunately, populations of some owls and woodpeckers, including the Eastern Screech-Owl and Red-bellied Woodpecker, are stable along much of the East Coast.

Other owls and woodpeckers, including the Barn Owl, Great Horned Owl, Red-headed Woodpecker, Hairy Woodpecker, Downy Woodpecker, and Yellow-bellied Sapsucker, also can find appropriate habitat in some urban and suburban areas of the East Coast.

Unable to create their own nests, secondary cavity nesters like this eastern bluebird benefit from holes abandoned by Northern Flickers.

9

Northeastern Forests

Fall in the Northeast brings a visual feast of red, yellow, purple, and orange foliage as shorter days and colder temperatures strip dozens of species of deciduous trees of their ability to synthesize chlorophyll, the green photosynthetic leaf pigment that converts light into sugars and starches necessary for growth, flowering, and production of seeds. In the absence of chlorophyll, carotene pigments color leaves yellow, while anthocyanin pigments interact with sugars to produce various shades of red and purple.

These brilliant fall colors abound throughout the deciduous and mixed deciduous-conifer forests of the northeastern states and the Appalachian Mountains. **Yellow-bellied Sapsuckers** create most of their sap wells in the most sucrose rich of these trees, including aspen, birch, and several species of maple, which also happen to be among the most colorful components of New England's famous fall color. This sapsucker serves as the keystone species for the region, both for its excavations, which are used by other cavity nesters, and for its sap wells, which provide access to energy-rich tree sap for a variety of mammals, insects, and birds, including the ruby-throated hummingbird.

At sap wells created by Yellow-bellied Sapsuckers in the southern Appalachians, I observed two birds alternating between three trees checkered with sap. In turn, each would land below a grid of rectangular wells and begin lapping up the overflowing sap. From there, the birds meticulously traced each rectangular hole with their bills, consuming every bit of sap, trapped insects, and even parts of the tree underneath the bark, thereby enlarging the wells. Once at the top, a new row of horizontal slits was carved just above the top wells. Over repeated visits this, too, was carved to a rectangular shape. Occasionally a ruby-throated hummingbird, yellow-rumped warbler, rival Yellow-bellied Sapsucker, or butterfly would visit the well, only to be swiftly repelled with loud squeals and waves of the sapsucker's bill. Wasps, on the other hand, were dealt with quite differently. When a wasp approached, the sapsucker would lean back with its head upside down and facing backward, its claws holding tightly and its tail pressed against the tree for balance. The wasp's path was tracked with bobbing head and snapping bill, before it was dispatched with a quick bite.

The Yellow-bellied Sapsucker is a medium-size, black-and-white woodpecker with a red crown on both sexes and a red chin on the male. The belly may have some yellow, but this varies greatly between birds. Two other closely related sapsuckers are differentiated by the pattern of their red adornment: the Red-naped Sapsucker has a red patch at the back of the neck, and the Red-breasted has a red head and red breast. The ranges

Opposite: After hearing another Barred Owl call, this male flies to investigate.

Yellow-bellied Sapsucker wells provide sap for Ruby-throated hummingbirds.

of the three species overlap slightly, and they have at times been considered one species.

The Yellow-bellied Sapsucker is North America's most migratory woodpecker, breeding from New England north and east across the northeastern and north-central states throughout much of the boreal forest and wintering from the southeastern United States through Central America. These populations appear to be stable, with perhaps higher popula- tions than existed during precolonial times, when northeastern North America was comprised of more old-growth forests. Small, isolated breeding populations are also found in the southern Appalachians.

Yellow-bellied Sapsuckers most commonly breed in de- ciduous and mixed-conifer forests along riparian zones up to 6,000 feet. Unlike most woodpeckers, these sapsuckers prefer young forests with colonizing deciduous trees for nesting and

Opposite: A female Yellow-bellied Sapsucker licks the sap from one of her wells.

feeding and thus are common in areas that have been cut or disturbed, while absent from dense conifer stands. During winter these birds favor forest edges, fruit trees, and other open habitats where sap is available.

Sap is the most important food for Yellow-bellied Sapsuckers, making up 20 percent of their food annually and nearly 100 percent during certain periods. Their tongues are equipped with a brush-like tip that aids in the collection of sap. Insects—with ants representing a significant part of the mix—and fruit, tree cambium, and other plant parts comprise the remainder of their diet. Their food

A Yellow-bellied Sapsucker traces the flight of a wasp attracted to its sweet sap-wells.

choices vary greatly by time of year, and nestlings eat primarily insects. Adults sometimes dip insects in sap before offering them to their young.

Male Yellow-bellied Sapsuckers arrive in their breeding range as early as late March and as late as early May, usually showing up in New Hampshire, Vermont, and Maine in early April. Upon arriving, males drill holes in parallel horizontal rows through the bark of deciduous trees into the xylem tissue where they feed upon the liquid (mostly water and minerals with some sucrose) moving upward from the roots.

As new buds form on quaking aspens and other trees, these sapsuckers are known to climb to the ends of branches to consume this treat. Once the trees leaf out, phloem tissue transports a richer sugary liquid from the leaves to the rest of the tree. Wells drilled into the phloem layer are the prime source of food during this time and are carefully maintained and guarded.

The ruby-throated hummingbird, the only hummingbird nesting east of the Mississippi River, binds itself in many ways to these sap wells, often nesting close to them and following the Yellow-bellied Sapsucker throughout the day as it retaps wells. In the northern parts of its range, the migrating ruby-throated hummingbird might be dependent upon these sap wells when it arrives, as few plants are producing nectar at that time of year.

Yellow-bellied Sapsuckers excavate most of their cavities in quaking aspen, preferring specimens infected with the heartwood decay fungus. Their nest cavities are so small that adult birds often lose feathers due to wear at the cavity's edges and usually look quite scraggy early in the nesting season. They often partially excavate several cavities before nesting in a final one. They frequently reuse nest trees for several consecutive years, and sometimes even reuse the same nest cavities.

Like other sapsuckers, the Yellow-bellied announces itself with a squeal-like mewing call and a drumming that starts with a burst of rapid taps followed by a gradually slowing beat with occasional double taps.

Old-growth deciduous-coniferous mixed forests of the eastern states, particularly moist bottomlands, are also ideal habitat for the **Barred Owl**, which serves as one of this habitat's indicator species. The Barred Owl occurs throughout older mixed forests in the eastern half of the United States and in the southern part of the boreal forest in Canada and has recently invaded the Pacific Northwest, where it has become quite com-

A Barred Owl calls for his mate.

mon, even nesting in several city parks in and around Seattle and threatening populations of Northern Spotted Owls elsewhere. The northern limits of its range are probably set by its ability to find prey during winter.

The Barred Owl is a medium-size gray to brown owl that can

The mixed forests of the Great North Woods provide habitat for the Yellow-bellied Sapsucker and the Northern Saw-whet Owl as well as other species of owls and woodpeckers.

be recognized by its large rounded head, distinctive facial disk, horizontal barring on the throat, and vertical bars on its breast. It looks much like its close relative, the Northern Spotted Owl, but is slightly larger and lacks spots on its breast. Also like its kin, this common owl benefits from greater availability of nest snags with broken tops or natural cavities, lower tree density, which facilitates hunting, and closed canopy for thermoregulation. Unlike the Spotted Owl it utilizes mature second-growth

forests in the Pacific Northwest. Although broken-topped trees and cavities are their preferred nest sites, Barred Owls will also use the stick nests of other birds and nest boxes. Barred Owls are for the most part monogamous and nonmigratory and will often breed in the same nest with the same mate for several consecutive years.

An opportunistic nocturnal owl, the Barred hunts a wide variety of prey, from small mammals to medium-size birds, as

The male Yellow-bellied Sapsucker possesses a red throat patch.

well as amphibians, reptiles, and even fish. This is a sit-and-wait predator that hunts from a tree branch or other perch using strong nocturnal vision (equal to that of the Barn Owl and Long-eared Owl) and precise hearing to locate prey. When capturing fish or crayfish, it might drop from a perch into the water or even wade in, pursuing its target.

One of the noisiest owls, the Barred has a variety of calls, from the widely known call phoneticized as *Who Cooks for You, Who Cooks for You All* to extremely loud barking and caterwauling that sound like no other owl I have heard.

An old observation that the call of another owl is reminiscent of the sound produced by filing the teeth of a large saw provides the name of the **Northern Saw-whet Owl.** Although birders disagree about which of the Saw-whet's calls that refers to, it might be the advertising call, which consists of a regular and constant series of whistled notes.

A small nocturnal owl, the Northern Saw-whet hunts the older coniferous forests of New England and the Appalachians. It has a very large, round head that lacks ear tufts, and its facial disk is distinctive and round with a Y-shaped marking formed by the cream-colored feathers above and between its yellow eyes. The breasts of adult birds are brown streaked with white, and their legs are densely feathered all the way to the talons.

Northern Saw-whet Owls breed in the southern boreal forests and the northern parts of New England, the Great Lakes, and the West Coast. They also breed throughout the western mountains and spottily in the Appalachians. During winter, large numbers of these owls migrate south, where they might end up roosting in dense thickets or perched hidden under the shelter of thick conifer limbs in any of the contiguous states. When found in these situations, Northern Saw-whets allow close approach, but care must be taken, as a flushed Northern Saw-whet might soon be another bird's meal.

Although usually monogamous, males are sometimes polygynous, raising broods with two females when food sources are plentiful. Some evidence indicates that females can be polyandrous, letting one mate raise their brood after leaving to raise another brood with another male.

Northern Saw-whet Owls hunt from perches where they wait for prey to pass. Like several other North American owls, they have asymmetrical skulls that result in asymmetrical, or offset, ears. The offset ears enable them to locate prey with their hearing alone. They capture prey with their feet and tear it into pieces, usually starting with the head. Small rodents, such as deer mice, shrews, and voles, are the favored prey, although they occasionally take birds.

Although Northern Saw-whets do not require old-growth forests, they require cavities such as those made by Northern Flickers and Pileated Woodpeckers, and the snags that host these are far more common in mature forests. Fortunately, these owls will use nest boxes when woodpecker cavities are not available.

Logging is the primary threat to habitat in this northeastern forested region. Acid rain, climate change, and the development of residential and recreational areas also pose challenges. More optimistically, much of the Northeast that had been converted to farmland during the nineteenth century has returned once again to forest during the past hundred years. The lessons learned since then should help the populations of owls, woodpeckers, and other animals in this region.

Opposite: A Northern Saw-whet Owl clutches a partially consumed deer mouse.

10

Boreal Forest

The boreal forest is a vast verdant blanket wrapped around the upper latitudes of the Northern Hemisphere across much of Alaska, Canada, Scandinavia, and Russia. While it is easy to think of the boreal as a huge, uniform swath of trees, in reality it is a mosaic of innumerable hues and textures of green and blue, cast by many species of spruce, birch, aspen, and pine, interwoven with more than one and a half million lakes and ponds, as well as burns and other natural openings.

The boreal forest is ecologically and visually analogous to the beautiful subalpine areas of the western mountains with which it shares several species of owls and woodpeckers, including the Boreal, Northern Saw-whet, and Great Gray Owls, and the Three-toed and Black-backed Woodpeckers. In both areas, stunted trees of various ages endure a harsh climate, but in the case of the boreal, this distinctive landscape stretches for thousands of miles.

The word *boreal* is derived from the name of the Greek god of the north wind, Boreas, who was depicted as strong and winged. More than 300 species of birds breed in the boreal forest, including more than 2 billion birds that wing south before the north wind becomes too fierce. More than a billion of these birds winter in the United States.

Thick blankets of sphagnum moss cushioned my steps through tall, reflective quaking aspens and heavily scented white and black spruce, and the low, soft Alaska summer light was hypnotic as I weaved through the boreal forest near Fairbanks searching for **Boreal Owls**. As I approached one promising nest site, a female squeezed her head out of the cavity, peering at me suspiciously before fleeing. Moments later this protective bird returned and a staccato trill above startled me—a haunting nocturnal voice in the daylight. Looking like all head and wings, the male weaved through the aspen, a plump, furry root vole in its bill, and landed on a nearby branch. Despite my presence, this Boreal was determined to bring food to the nest. Impatient, it shifted, switching the vole from bill to talons. After photographing a few images I retreated, not wanting to deter the mission, and witnessed from a distance as the owl surged to the nest, wings and talons leading the way.

The Boreal Owl is relatively small, its large head featuring a prominent grayish facial disk framed by a dark border. It is distinguished from its relative the Northern Saw-whet Owl by its larger size, as well as by white spots on its brown crown and a light-colored bill in contrast to white streaking on the lighter-brown crown and dark-colored bill of the Northern Saw-whet. All North American owls have reverse sexual dimorphism, with females being larger than males. The Boreal shows the most extreme example of

Opposite: A male Boreal Owl prepares to deliver a root vole to his mate waiting with their young.

During the winter, Great Gray Owls travel in search of food, sometimes showing up in pastures and other rural landscapes.

A fledgling Boreal Owl scrambles through leaf litter on the forest floor.

reverse sexual dimorphism, with females weighing approximately 40 percent more than males.

In North America, the Boreal Owl occurs throughout the boreal forests of Alaska and Canada, in forests of the northernmost points of several of the Lower 48 states, and in isolated subalpine mountain pockets in the Pacific Northwest and Rocky Mountains into northern New Mexico. The winter range is identical to the breeding range, except during irruption years of food scarcity that drive some of the boreal populations into southern provinces and

northern states. The Boreal Owl's prime habitat in Alaska and Canada is comprised of black and white spruce with pockets of aspen, poplar, birch, and balsam fir. Where its range extends into northern parts of states such as Minnesota, Michigan, and Maine, it inhabits areas with aspen and a mix of other trees. In its isolated subalpine populations, its typical habitat often includes mountain hemlock, Engelmann spruce, subalpine fir, and lodgepole pine.

Voles of various species, particularly red-backed and heather voles, are the prime food for the Boreal Owl, although it will

Opposite: With the rising moon behind him, a Northern Hawk Owl uses his keen eyesight to look for prey.

Great Gray Owls take advantage of forest openings, like those created by burns, to hunt for rodents.

they are in low years, and these fluctuations are not predictable. Higher vole populations have been shown to result in larger Boreal Owl clutch sizes, and larger clutch sizes produce more fledglings. During winter, Boreal Owls prefer to hunt within the forest where the snow is less likely to have a frozen crust and prey is thus more readily accessible, while during spring they may hunt in more open areas.

From the time that a pair of Boreals mates until the young fledge, pressure is extreme to meet caloric needs, first of the mother to maximize clutch size and then of the young to prevent starvation and to speed up maturation. Ample food supply can ensure similar growth rates of all young and move the fledging date up by a day or two, sometimes making the difference between life and death for the young, who are otherwise subject to predation in the nest.

The road to fledging can appear to be a brutal race for the owls. Watching nests outside Fairbanks, I felt the tension and urgency of males as they delivered voles to their nests. These owls begin accumulating voles in the nest cavities before the eggs are hatched and deliver as many as possible through fledging; it is not uncommon to see dead voles lying beside the eggs and owlets. The owlets grow fast, and their food demands increase. If the parents do not provide enough food, hunger can drive them to devour their siblings. During this time, the cavities are full of odor and sound, luring hungry predators, usually martens, although I once saw the distinctive claw marks of a lynx leading up to a nest.

Nocturnal, except during twenty-four-hour light in the northern parts of its range, the Boreal Owl moves in a zigzag pattern from perch to perch throughout its territory, waiting for prey. Often, these owls will spot prey and watch it, waiting for it to move into a more vulnerable position before striking. Targeted prey is usually quite close to the current perch.

Of all North American owls, Boreal Owls have the most extremely asymmetrical skulls and offset ears, which allow for the precise localization of sounds in vertical and horizontal directions and enable them to locate prey under snow or hidden in vegetation. During winter, they frequently cache their prey near a roost or inside the empty nest cavity.

Several different calls have been described for the Boreal Owl, although the most common one consists of a series of trills of the same frequency that increase in volume. A pause of several seconds often occurs before this call is repeated. The call is

prey upon mice and other small mammals, birds, and even insects. Given its reliance upon voles, the irruptive nature of vole populations has profound impacts upon the survival and reproduction of Boreals from year to year. In the boreal forests, vole populations can be twenty times higher in irruptive years than

After detecting prey, a Great Gray Owl launches a silent hunt.

A Northern Hawk Owl snaps from a perched position into a dive.

After pouncing upon prey hidden under the snow, Great Gray Owls often look stunned before taking flight again.

only given during the breeding season and is used by the male to advertise a potential nest cavity.

The Boreal Owl is considered a "sensitive species" in several areas of the United States and Canada, due in large part to its reliance upon older forests. Trees grow slowly in both the boreal and subalpine areas, and a nest tree must be large enough to accommodate the Northern Flicker or Pileated Woodpecker cavities that this obligate cavity nester typically requires. Northern Flickers occur throughout its range, but Pileated Woodpeckers do not live in the northern boreal or in

the subalpine areas of the southern Rocky Mountains. Fortunately, the Boreal Owl will utilize nest boxes, sometimes even in consecutive years, if boxes are cleaned and maintained by the researchers, scientists, or volunteers who install them.

The limited supply of large woodpecker cavities and the irruptive nature of the Boreal Owl's food supply are the primary limits on its population. Large swaths of the boreal forest are being cut, and such cuts usually remove the larger nest and roosting trees and eliminate the forest structure necessary for foraging. After a clear-cut, young trees can require up to 200 years to grow to a size large enough to support a cavity. Selective cutting and thinning can be done in a way that minimizes these risks.

Although many owls breed in the boreal forest, often nesting and hunting similar prey in close proximity to one another, their ideal habitats differ. The **Great Gray Owl** lives in more open forests than the Boreal Owl, and although it also hunts from perches, it is more likely to fly a greater distance to capture prey, sometimes even hunting by wing over fields in daylight.

One frigid winter morning just south of the boreal in northern Minnesota, the thermometer read minus twenty degrees Fahrenheit and the clock read 5:00 AM, but the thrill of a chance to photograph the Great Gray Owl hunting made these circumstances seem like minor inconveniences. I had watched her hunt the day before, noting her favored perches, angle and height of pursuit, where the sun rose and set, when the first light hit the snow, and when certain portions of the field were shaded. Knowing this owl was an auditory hunter, I knew I would have to choose one spot and remain still to avoid interfering with her efforts to pursue prey near me.

I trudged through the snow to a spot where the drifts hugged mid-thigh. For hours I waited and hoped, watching the owl sit on a single perch in the meadow. A launch, a dive, and a failed attack drove her back into the air and, fortunately for me, eventually to my predicted treetop. I knew there would be one critical fraction of a second to capture her launch from the tree, and if I missed it, I would have little chance of tracking her across the field with my camera. From that moment on I struggled to hold my arms up and my finger poised in the fierce cold. To poise my finger, my whole hand had to be exposed to the icy wind—how could a finger feel so heavy? The owl launched as I had hoped, toward a vole she had heard near me. Shortly after the launch she slowed abruptly, hovered, and plunged headfirst into the snow, flattening as she hit the surface. Alarmed by her sprawling appearance, I rushed over to assist her. She turned her head and fixed me with her intense gaze, warning me not to approach. Slowly she pulled her wings in, raised her body and lifted into the air, vole in talons, then disappeared into the woods.

The Great Gray Owl, or Great Gray Ghost as it is sometimes called, truly seems to be a spirit of these northern woods. Its species name *nebulosa*, derived from the Latin word for "misty" or "foggy," hints at its appearance. It sometimes appears more apparition than bird, as its sooty color blends into the lichen-encrusted bark and gray, leafless trees of winter, particularly during the dusk, evening, and dawn hours when it hunts.

Great Gray Owls look massive, and they are, in fact, the longest North American owl at twenty-seven inches. They also share

Cooper's hawks, along with the two other Northern American accipiters—goshawks and sharp-shinned hawks—are among the primary predators of woodpeckers and small owls.

A Great Gray Owl considers his surroundings.

with the Snowy Owl the longest wingspan of fifty-two inches; however, their average weight of 2.4 pounds is significantly less than the Snowy Owl's 4.1 pounds and the Great Horned Owl's 3.1 pounds. Much of their bulk is made up of thick feathers that enable survival in the harsh northern winters. Females are on the average more than a third larger than males.

The Great Gray's long body and wingspan result in low wing loading, which allows a surprisingly agile and silent flight when hunting. Its feathers are soft and flexible and thus are rarely injured when it weaves through the trunks and branches of its forest hideouts.

I am amazed every time I see this owl. The sheer size is something expected from a mammal, not a bird. Rather than fleeing, this owl often stares from its bowl-like face and small golden eyes, as if fascinated. When it finally decides to fly, it falls onto the air like a box kite and slowly floats to a new perch.

After leaping down from its cavity at the top of a snag, a fledgling Northern Hawk Owl runs across a downed log.

If the day is cold and the light is low, it will not let your presence deter it from hunting in a field, marsh, burnt landscape, or forest opening.

Like the Boreal Owl, the Great Gray Owl has an asymmetrical skull with offset ears that allow it to precisely locate prey such as voles and lemmings up to twelve inches deep in snow. Its head bobs from side to side as it searches the audioscape for prey. When it catches the sound of a rodent moving below the snow, it turns its head toward something invisible. If wind ruffles its feathers or sways the branch it is on, its head remains still. When it attacks, as I discovered, it seems to fall face first through the snow and ice.

In actuality, the Great Gray Owl launches its attack talons first, drawing its long, powerful legs forward under its chin as it crashes through snow and ice sheets thick enough to carry a 180-pound person, seizing its microtine (vole) prey. It takes a few moments to pull its prey and its own body back up through the snow and ice and clear its wings of the snow before lifting off.

This owl is for the most part a bird of dense, northern boreal forests, where it hunts at edges of open spaces, such as sphagnum bogs, muskegs, and burns. It is found in much of Alaska and Canada with range extensions into northern states and western mountains. In the southern part of its range, the Great Gray is a year-round resident, sometimes moving to lower elevations when snow is deep at its usual high-elevation haunts. In the northern part of its range, it is irruptive. During irruption winters, when the availability of prey lures it south, great numbers are found in forest openings, prairie provinces, the Great Lakes states, and even northeast New England, where it sometimes hunts during the day to survive winter.

Northern Minnesota experienced one such irruption during the winter of 2004–2005 when more than 2,000 owls descended upon an area where fewer than 40 owls are found in most winters. It seemed that every field, swamp, and forest opening had a good chance of hosting at least one Great Gray Owl.

This normally nocturnal owl typically hunts small mammals, with voles being the primary food throughout most of its range. Pocket gophers are a significant prey of Great Gray Owls in more southern areas, such as Idaho, Wyoming, and northern California. It also sometimes consumes birds, such as sharp-shinned hawks, broad-winged hawks, jays, and grouse.

This female Boreal Owl is much larger than her mate but is otherwise indistinguishable from him.

The Great Gray uses abandoned nests of hawks and other raptors, broken-topped snags, mistletoe brooms, and even human-made platforms as nest sites. It adds nothing to these platforms, although the female may scratch a depression at

Relying upon his amazing hearing, a Great Gray Owl tilts his facial disk in order to accurately pinpoint the location of a vole moving beneath the snow.

A Northern Hawk Owl delivers food to his pleading fledgling.

the bottom before laying her eggs. These owls, particularly females, defend their nests ferociously, and their attacks have reportedly inflicted serious injuries on people and driven away even bears.

As might be expected of a seminomadic owl, Great Gray pair bonds are not usually maintained and nests are not often used in successive years, although exceptions occur when the food supply is high, particularly in southern parts of its range.

Juveniles disperse widely at times but at other times stay to breed very close to where they fledge.

The Great Gray Owl is one of the least vocal of all owls. Its most common territorial call is a series of several extremely low, muffled, regularly spaced *hoos*.

The greatest threat to Great Gray populations is timber harvesting, as that often reduces the number of large-diameter trees and snags used for nesting, leaning trees used by juveniles for preflight roosting, and dense stands that protect juveniles. To remain hospitable to this owl, clear-cuts must leave perches for hunting in the open and have irregularly shaped edges.

The population density of Great Gray Owls is limited by the availability of food and nest sites, so if timber harvests are not too intense and retain the aforementioned features, the addition of human-made nest structures might help retain populations. Such nest structures are readily accepted and sometimes chosen over previously used nest sites, provided they are in forested stands, rather than at the edge of a clearing or clear-cut, and face north to maximize shade. Small cut areas might actually enhance habitat by creating hunting areas in otherwise dense stands.

As it spends much more time in openings of marshes, muskegs, and burns, the **Northern Hawk Owl** prefers conifer and mixed-conifer parts of the boreal that are more open than those

With several gulps, a fledgling Northern Hawk Owl consumes a vole.

An aggressive hunter, the Northern Hawk Owl is frequently indifferent to the presence of people.

Black spruce, white spruce, aspen, and birch are major components of the boreal forest.

denser woods preferred by the Boreal and Great Gray Owls. These settings feature the tall, isolated perches utilized by this visual hunter.

I found a Northern Hawk Owl in a burn in the boreal forest of northern Alberta. Perched atop the highest snag in a burned forest opening, long tail descending at forty-five degrees, head leaning forward, small yellow eyes slowly scanning the ground, he could not be confused with any other owl. Abruptly, his head snapped down into position, his body stiffened, and his tail pumped up and eased down before he exploded into an accelerating, near-vertical dive, head straight down, wings tight against his body. He spread his wings and flattened his course inches above the ground, whipping around trees, then striking and lifting a vole in one fluid movement without deceleration, completing his distinctive U-shaped course with a steep climb to the top of another snag.

A bold, medium-size diurnal (active in the daylight) owl, the Northern Hawk Owl indeed looks remarkably like a hawk. At rest, it rarely sits erect like other owls, and in flight it is swift and agile, with a pointed wing profile like that of a Cooper's hawk.

The majority of breeding populations of Northern Hawk Owls live within the boreal forests, where they breed from the southern fringes to the edge of the tree line. Unlike many boreal birds and all other boreal owls, their regular breeding range does not extend into the western mountain ranges that offer boreal-like habitat in the Lower 48 states. It is possible that their daytime activity would require too much competition with other diurnal raptors in more southerly mountains. Winters find this nomadic owl moving into southern Canada and the northern states, particularly during irruption years.

Like other nomadic birds, the Northern Hawk Owl often surprises. In addition to irruptions in northern Minnesota and in the boreal forest north of Winnipeg, I photographed one outside its described winter range near Bend, Oregon, as well as a family south of its expected breeding range in northwestern Montana. Although unexpected, both sightings were in areas with this owl's critical habitat elements: a rich supply of voles, prominent perches, and an open area in which to hunt. Both habitats were the result of forest fires.

Throughout the Northern Hawk Owl's range, fire is a common precursor to proper habitat, as it can open formerly dense forests, creating an environment hospitable to rodents, a better landscape for visual hunters, and snags in which to nest and from which to hunt. Nest sites are often near water, where prey is more abundant.

Despite having a symmetrical skull without the offset ears of other auditory hunters, the Northern Hawk Owl has excellent hearing, which allows it to detect and capture prey located almost a foot under snow cover. That said, this owl relies more upon its extraordinary vision to locate prey. With tall snags and open hunting habitat, it is able to detect prey almost a half mile away.

The availability of prey drives the wanderings of the Northern Hawk Owl. As with other northern owls, voles are its most important food, although it eats other small mammals and birds, particularly when voles are less accessible under heavy snow cover. Boreal prey populations are unstable, as they are impacted by natural population irruptions, snow cover, and other climatic factors. Vole population cycles vary geographically, but when voles decline regionwide, these owls must move south to find food. If food is abundant, they may stay and breed in more southern locations, resulting in a temporary range extension.

The species name *ulula* is derived from the Latin *ululare*, "to cry" or "to scream," and reflects the rapid, high-pitched trill *ulululu* that a Northern Hawk Owl emits when advertising its territory at the beginning of breeding season. During winter, however, this owl falls silent.

Northern Hawk Owls usually nest in tree cavities. In the southern part of their breeding range, their habitat overlaps with that of the Pileated Woodpecker, whose cavities provide good nest sites, but a large proportion of nests are situated in natural cavities in the broken tops of large trees. Sometimes they use the abandoned nests of ravens or hawks.

As with most owls, the female incubates the eggs and broods young while the male provides food. While observing a Northern Hawk Owl family in the Canadian Rockies, I learned that a loud, raspy, two-part screech—*scree-yip*—indicated that the male was arriving with a food delivery. As the owlets grew older, the female would fly to meet the male at a nearby snag, receive the food, and fly to the nest to feed only the owlets that were vocalizing. If they were silent, the food was cached. The cache sites included old woodpecker holes and the crooks of trees where branches met the trunk.

The young leave the nest at three to five weeks of age, when they jump, fall, or flutter to the ground, with the whole brood usually fledging over a period of several days. I was surprised by how quickly and independently the young dispersed upon fledging. Each owlet repeated the same process: a long fall from the nest, followed by solo explorations in which every short vertical structure, be it branch, slab of bark, or stump, was tenaciously scaled using various combinations of bill, talons, and wings, and then used for launching. Occasionally, an exhausted owlet settled its feathered weight upon the bark and took a break. At other times, after reaching a peak, it would scream for food, forcing a parent to land upon odd branches or even the vertical face of a strip of bark to feed it. After a few days, the small owls were able to clumsily fly twenty to thirty feet at a time.

Northern Hawk Owls are quite solitary outside the breeding

Each of these Northern Hawk Owl siblings hatched on a different day and thus each shows slightly different plumage.

season, so although they are monogamous, pair bonds end shortly after the young disperse. Like other nomadic owls they do not show fidelity to mates or nest sites over consecutive years.

Much of the boreal forest is being cut and tree plantations established. Both clear-cuts and plantations are detrimental in that they often remove hunting and nesting snags, but clear-cuts also can offer benefits in increased vole populations and open areas for hunting. The state of Northern Hawk Owl populations is uncertain. The heart of this bird's habitat is the more open northern boreal forest once considered to be noncommercial. However, the boreal is now being cut so fast that this description may no longer be accurate.

The boreal forest region of North America alone encompasses 1.5 billion acres and comprises 25 percent of the world's remaining intact forest. This forest helps ameliorate the impact of global warming by storing massive amounts of carbon, yet less than 10 percent of the Canadian boreal forests are protected. As consumers, we can help protect boreal habitat by making conscious purchasing decisions. Millions of acres of virgin boreal forest are harvested annually in part to produce such pedestrian products as junk mail and tissue paper. By requesting postconsumer recycled paper products, reducing junk mail, and purchasing only sustainably harvested (FSC certified) lumber, we can help promote more sustainable choices that conserve habitat for owls—and the many other birds of the boreal forests.

11

Arctic Tundra

The Inupiat name for the town of Barrow, Alaska, is Ukpiagvik, which means "the place where we hunt Snowy Owls." Before embarking on my own hunt for these ghostly birds, I knew I would be spending days at a time taking photos from a blind on the tundra and was concerned about being hunted myself by polar bears. I had been reassured that the ice would be out during the time of year I would be there and that polar bears only hunt when the ice is in. I arrived to a wet, cold, windy harbor with thick sheets of ice abutting the land, definitely not "out." Concerned, I inquired of a stoic Inupiat man, "Will bears wander the tundra today?" He replied, "It depends what the bear decides." Not satisfied with the answer, I posed the same question to an older, more approachable native, and he answered matter of factly, "It is up to the bear." I realized that in the Arctic it is difficult to predict nature, and I would have to respond to unforeseen opportunities and challenges as best I could, just as the Snowy Owl does.

The **Snowy Owl**, the heaviest and longest-winged North American owl, is a white-feathered relative of the Great Horned Owl. Males are almost pure white with small brown specks, juveniles are covered with dark bars and markings, and females are somewhere in between. Once considered to be in its own genus, *Nyctea*, Snowy Owls are now grouped together with the Great Horned Owl in the genus *Bubo*. With their great size (mature females can weigh up to five pounds), Snowy Owls are able to carry more insulation in their feathers and possess the lowest thermal conductance among all birds, equivalent to that of arctic foxes and Dall sheep.

This circumpolar species breeds on the tundra, the treeless plain that extends from the edge of the polar seas to near tree line. From a distance the Arctic tundra appears to be an undulating golden-green carpet cut by lakes, canals, ponds, and wetlands of various depths. At closer inspection, it is a soggy weave of grasses, sedges, liverworts, and mosses that are eaten by musk ox, caribou, and lemmings; the latter, in turn, provide food for several other animals, including arctic foxes, Short-eared Owls, and Snowy Owls.

Winters find Snowy Owls moving south through Canada and the northern United States, particularly the northern Great Plains. Periodic irruption years bring exponential increases in the number of birds found in these more southern areas. The most common explanation is that the birds are responding to a fall in lemming populations to the north, although the lemming cycles and Snowy Owl irruptions are not always directly correlated.

When winter sets in, females retain the breeding territories; males and juveniles migrate south, with juvenile males

Opposite: As the sun sets behind her, a Snowy Owl becomes more alert to take advantage of available rodents.

traveling farthest. Males often arrive first in wintering areas but may eventually be displaced by the more dominant females, who move south when resources become scarce in their home territories. The final winter distribution from Arctic summer grounds to the primary wintering areas of the Great Plains finds adult females farthest north and immature males farthest south, with adult males and immature females somewhere in between. The Snowy Owl visitors to the East and West Coasts are mostly made up of irruptive first-year birds.

The wanderings of these birds are unpredictable, with members of a single clutch moving far and wide after fledging. For example, seven siblings were banded in 1962 on Victoria Island in the Northwest Territories. Within a seven-month period the following year, three of them were recovered: one in eastern Ontario, one near Hudson Bay, and the third in eastern Siberia.

Snowy Owls are dependent primarily upon lemmings as a food source during their breeding season in the Arctic; in

Like other owls of open landscapes, Snowy Owls hunt on the wing.

A female Snowy Owl confronts a pomarine jaeger on the Arctic tundra.

the southern wintering areas, voles and rabbits are the prey of choice. Their diets in the Arctic are supplemented by ducks, geese, jaegers, shorebirds, longspurs, and even weasels. During their winter wanderings, they further expand their diets to include rats, mice, and other birds and small mammals. Foxes and pomerine jaegers sometimes attack Snowy Owls for food, and wolves and dogs probably do as well.

Occasionally, Snowy Owls will pair up in winter grounds and migrate north together; at other times they establish pairs once they reach the breeding territory. They are fairly monogamous, but as might be expected of nomadic animals, season-to-season pair bonds are weak.

Snowy Owls choose nest sites that are exposed and elevated on an otherwise flat landscape. These sites are the first to be free of snow and moisture and offer views of the surrounding landscape with room to escape without being noticed, should a predator approach. Often these sites are close to water where lemming populations are high.

Once a nest site is chosen, the female will scratch and claw and spin until a shallow hollow, called a scrape, is created in the ground. Although nothing is added to these nests, the depression eventually accumulates feathers, droppings, and remains of prey. Over time, debris in the nest and in other places where Snowy Owls eat provides nutrients to the soil, creating an oasis of greenery and flowers in an otherwise muted landscape. These green areas often attract voles and may later become the fertile hunting areas of other animals, such as arctic foxes, Short-eared Owls, or even other Snowy Owls. The owls sometimes

The youngest Snowy Owl chick is just visible from between its older siblings.

reuse their scrapes as nest sites. Interestingly, some birds that are potential prey, such as eiders and geese, will nest very close to a Snowy Owl nest, somehow knowing that the owls aggressively defend their nests against potential predators and many do not hunt close to their own nests.

Lemming populations in the Arctic are highly unpredictable and irruptive, and Snowy Owls sometimes go many seasons without breeding when lemming populations are low. Somehow these nomadic owls seem to know when and where the lemming season will be rich and show up in large numbers to take advantage of the opportunities. Even in the most predictable spots, however, Snowy Owl breeding is extremely unpredictable. In one area in the Arctic, for example, there were no nests in 2004, fewer than five in 2005, more than thirty-five in 2006, and none in 2007.

The number of eggs laid by the female depends largely on the availability of lemmings, and the presentation of a lemming by the male to the female during courtship is a signal for the females that initiates breeding pair formation. When lemming populations are very low, no eggs are laid. In somewhat more populous years, the female might lay three to five eggs, while peak lemming years often yield seven to eleven eggs. Clutches of as many as sixteen eggs have been reported. Eggs are laid asynchronously with as many as four days between eggs, although two days between eggs is most common. Owlets typically leave the nest when they are twenty-five days old, although they do not fly until they are about forty-five days old.

In Barrow, I was surprised to find a successful brood with two youngsters that had already left the nest and appeared to be near fledging, while several small fluffy white siblings nestled with an even younger pinkish owlet. This developmental staggering likely offers a survival advantage to a species with an unpredictable climate and food supply.

Although North America's heaviest owl, the Snowy Owl is a powerful flyer.

Mostly silent during winter, during the breeding season Snowy Owls utter several different calls. The most owl-like is described as a deep *hoo* followed by a stretched out *hooooo*. When I was watching them near Barrow, these fierce owls frequently issued another call before responding to a pomerine jaeger or trying to attack me. Each time I crested a hill and was in view of the male overseeing its territory, it flew into the air and, when my back was to him, all four pounds of muscle, feather, and bill dove at me with open, razor-sharp talons, screaming *ha, how, quack, quock,* or *guawk* over and over. The sun was at its back so I was unable to detect its shape or distance. At these times I crouched and hid underneath my tripod and large lens and quickly made progress after each near-miss, hoping I would not be among the many who have been severely injured by the talons of these aggressive birds.

Snowy Owls have long captivated humans. The image of a pair with a chick was etched into a cave in Les Trois Fréres, Ariége, in the French Pyrenees, and it is believed to be the oldest recognizable bird in prehistoric art. We have also been the Snowy's primary predators, however. Fortunately, most of the breeding population lies north of the reach of humans, and laws now prohibit taking these birds for food, sport, or trophies. Native peoples of the North can still harvest owls for food, feathers, and claws, but this is rare and is unlikely to have a significant impact on populations. We have no idea exactly how many Snowy Owls exist, nor do we know if their populations are stable or in decline. Since this owl is nomadic, migratory, irruptive, and responsive to irruptive prey populations, any significant change in its environment could have severe repercussions.

A female Snowy Owl's brood patch is visible as she returns to the nest.

In common with other large owls, the male Snowy Owl delivers food to the female who will distribute it to her young.

Climate change will likely have the most dramatic effect upon Snowy Owl populations. Lemmings, the owls' primary food, are herbivores, feeding upon the tundra sedges and mosses throughout the year, even during winter when they are insulated from the frigid Arctic cold by the snow that surrounds their burrows and tunnels. With the warmer weather brought by climate change, Arctic lakes are sustaining greater evaporation, which is drying the tundra and inhibiting growth of the plants upon which lemmings depend. The warmer climate is also allowing shrubs to displace these sedges and mosses. In addition, climate change is expected to bring warmer and more variable winters, which in turn will probably result in more freezing and thawing events. Cumulatively, these factors will likely make it more difficult for lemmings to recover from their periodic population crashes, which may destabilize and threaten the entire Arctic food web, including the already unpredictable populations of Snowy Owls.

The Arctic region has been one of the first regions of the world to show us the negative impacts of global warming. The fragile state of the Arctic tundra requires that we redouble our efforts to address climate change so we can save Snowy Owls and the other plants and animals of this ecosystem.

Next page: A female Snowy Owl with her young on the Arctic tundra.

Field Guide to North American Owl and Woodpecker Species

OWLS

North America hosts 19 owls from 2 different families and 10 genera, with all but the Barn Owl grouped in the same family. While owls are typically thought of as nocturnal, 7 North American owls are at least partly diurnal (active in daylight) or crepuscular (active at twilight). Most owls nest in cavities, with 10 species nesting in the cavities of woodpeckers.

Owls vary in weight from 1.2 ounces to 5 pounds, in length from 5.25 to 33 inches from top of head to tip of tail, and in wingspan from 12 to 52 inches. North American owls take advantage of a variety of habitats, from city parks to rain forests to dry deserts to the Arctic tundra. Some are sedentary, some are migratory, some are irruptive, and others are nomadic.

BARN OWL *(Tyto alba)*

Description: A medium-size buff-colored owl with a heart-shaped facial disk, approximately 16 inches long with a wingspan of 42 inches.

Similar Species: Unlikely to be confused with any other North American owl except in flight, when due to its light coloration one might mistake it for the larger and whiter Snowy Owl.

Interesting Fact: World's most widespread owl, and the one most adapted to living alongside humans.

North American Distribution and Habitat: Found in a wide variety of rural, urban, and suburban habitats throughout most states, barely reaching Canada in southwestern British Columbia.

Nesting: February until late November, nests in a variety of cavities including cliff banks, haystacks, barns, church steeples, nest boxes, and such. Lays 2 to 18 eggs, sometimes 2 or even 3 clutches in a season.

Vocalization: Most common call is a drawn out hissing scream, *sssssssshhh.*

SHORT-EARED OWL *(Asio flammeus)*

Description: A medium-size, long-winged, diurnal owl, approximately 15 inches long with a wingspan of 38 inches.

Similar Species: At rest, with or without small ear tufts displayed, it is distinctive, but in flight it can be confused with the darker Long-eared Owl that hunts at night.

Interesting Fact: Like the Long-eared Owl, known for "wing-clap" displays during courtship.

North American Distribution and Habitat: Breeds in open landscapes throughout much of the Arctic; boreal, interior West; Great Plains; and parts of California. Winters west, south, and east of these areas.

Nesting: Mid-March through late June, in a bowl scraped out of the ground by the female and lined with grasses. Lays 1 to 11 eggs.

Vocalization: Silent except during mating season, when a soft *voo-poo-poo-poo* is uttered over a few seconds.

LONG-EARED OWL *(Asio otus)*

Description: A medium-size long-winged owl with false ear tufts invisible in flight, approximately 15 inches long, with a wingspan of 36 inches.

Similar Species: At rest with ear tufts up it might be mistaken for the much larger Great Horned Owl, and in flight with invisible ear tufts it can be confused with the longer-winged and lighter-colored Short-eared Owl.

Interesting Fact: Roosts communally during the nonbreeding season with roosts of between 2 and 100 or so birds.

North American Distribution and Habitat: Breeds in lightly treed or open landscapes throughout much of Canada, the interior West, Great Plains, parts of California, and parts of the eastern states. Winters south and east of these areas and can be found in southern provinces in some summers.

Nesting: Late February through mid-July, in stick nests of other birds, in clumps of trees. Lays 2 to 10 eggs.

Vocalization: A series of soft, low *hooo* notes, with a couple of seconds between them. Several to more than a hundred notes can be heard in a row.

SNOWY OWL *(Bubo scandicus)*

Description: A large, long-winged white owl, approximately 23 inches long with a wingspan of 52 inches.

Similar Species: Heavily barred juveniles might be confused with whitish-colored Arctic forms of the Great Horned Owl.

Interesting Fact: A nomadic owl that may breed in different places from year to year and skip breeding altogether some years.

North American Distribution and Habitat: A year-round resident of the Arctic, with individuals that move south across the boreal region and even into the northern states in winter.

Nesting: Mid-May through late September, in a scrape scratched on the ground by the female, often on a mound. Lays 2 to 15 eggs that hatch on different days, so young of markedly different sizes can be seen in the same nest. Often reuses scrape.

Vocalization: *Hoo-hoo,* usually two parts but sometimes several.

GREAT HORNED OWL *(Bubo virginianus)*

Description: A large owl with distinctive ear tufts, approximately 22 inches long with a wingspan of 44 inches.

Similar Species: At rest, might be confused with the much smaller and more slender Long-eared Owl; whitish Arctic forms might be confused with heavily barred juvenile Snowy Owls.

Interesting Fact: Most widespread owl in North America, with significant regional color variation.

North American Distribution and Habitat: A year-round resident throughout most of the United States and Canada south of the tundra, including every state and province.

Nesting: Late February through late April, in nests of other raptors, or inside various cavities, including stick nests of other birds, cliff sides, tree cavities, or inside abandoned buildings. Lays 1 to 5 eggs.

Vocalization: Deep, foghorn-like *who-hoo-ho-ooo,* with variations.

GREAT GRAY OWL *(Strix nebulosa)*

Description: A large gray owl with a distinctive facial disk, small yellow eyes, approximately 27 inches long with a wingspan of 52 inches.

Similar Species: Larger and grayer than the Barred Owl or Spotted Owl. Yellow rather than black eyes.

Interesting Fact: The longest owl in North America.

North American Distribution and Habitat: A year-round resident of boreal forests of Canada and Alaska and western mountains that irrupts south into northern states.

Nesting: Late May through late July, in old stick nests of other raptors, on broken tops of trees, or on nest platforms. Lays 3 to 5 eggs. Often reuses nest for several years.

Vocalization: Series of low *hooos.*

SPOTTED OWL *(Strix occidentalis)*

Description: A medium-size brown owl with a spotted breast, approximately 17.5 inches long with a wingspan of 40 inches. Three subspecies found in North America.

Similar Species: Very similar in appearance to the slightly larger Barred Owl but distinguished by its spotted rather than streaked breast.

Interesting Fact: Hunts and roosts within the forest canopy. Northern subspecies population rapidly declining. Requires about 3,000 acres (0.5 to 0.75 mile per side) to meet food and nesting requirements.

North American Distribution and Habitat: A year-round resident of mature western forests, including those of the Pacific Coast and Southwest.

Nesting: Early March through mid-June, in tree cavities, old stick nests of another bird, squirrel nests, or mistletoe mats. Lays 1 to 4 eggs. Sometimes reuses nest cavities. Does not necessarily nest each year.

Vocalization: Like many owls, uses several vocalizations. Primary vocalization is a low-pitched series of *hoots* referred to as the "four-note location call," consisting of a single *hoot* with a short pause, two tightly placed *hoots,* and a final fading *hoot.*

BARRED OWL *(Strix varia)*

Description: A medium-size brown owl with a streaked breast, approximately 21 inches long with a wingspan of 42 inches.

Similar Species: Very similar in appearance to the slightly smaller Spotted Owl but distinguished by its streaked rather than spotted breast.

Interesting Fact: Expanding its range more than any other North American owl.

North American Distribution and Habitat: Year-round resident of eastern forests, parts of the boreal forest and northern Rockies, and the Pacific Northwest south to northern California.

Nesting: Mid-December through late September, in tree cavities, old stick nests of other birds, squirrel nests, or mistletoe mats. Lays 1 to 5 eggs. Often reuses nests.

Vocalization: Call phoneticized as *Who Cooks for You, Who Cooks for You All.*

NORTHERN SAW-WHET OWL *(Aegolius acadicus)*

Description: A small brown owl with a distinctive facial disk, approximately 8 inches long with a wingspan of 17 inches.

Similar Species: Very similar in appearance to larger Boreal Owl but smaller with more distinctive catlike white eyebrows.

Interesting Fact: Can locate prey through hearing alone.

North American Distribution and Habitat: A year-round resident of southern boreal, western, and northeastern forests, with wintering birds occasionally found throughout all but the most southern extremes of the United States.

Nesting: Early March through July, in Northern Flicker or Pileated Woodpecker cavities or in nest boxes. Lays 4 to 7 eggs.

Vocalization: A series of whistles of a single tone, with 2 seconds between each.

BOREAL OWL *(Aegolius funereus)*

Description: A small brown owl with a large head and distinctive facial disk, approximately 10 inches long with a wingspan of 21 inches.

Similar Species: Looks very much like the smaller Saw-whet Owl but larger with dark frame on face.

Interesting Fact: Females larger than males to a greater degree than any other North American owl.

North American Distribution and Habitat: Year-round resident of boreal forests, with isolated pockets in western mountains.

Nesting: Late March through July, in Northern Flicker or Pileated Woodpecker cavities or in nest boxes. Lays 2 to 5 eggs.

Vocalization: A trill comprised of whistled *toots.*

NORTHERN HAWK OWL *(Surnia ulula)*

Description: A medium-size brown owl, with a long tail, approximately 16 inches long with a wingspan of 28 inches.

Similar Species: Not likely to be confused with any other owl.

Interesting Fact: Hunts in the open, in the daylight, from exposed perches where it can spot prey from almost a half mile away.

North American Distribution and Habitat: A resident of the boreal forest up to the tree line, with periodic forays south into the northern states.

Nesting: Late March through August, in Pileated Woodpecker and natural cavities in trees or snags. Lays 3 to 13 eggs.

Vocalization: Rapid, high-pitched trill.

ELF OWL *(Micrathene whitneyi)*

Description: A small grayish-brown owl with yellow eyes, approximately 5.75 inches long with a wingspan of 13 inches.

Similar Species: Distinguished from the Flammulated Owl by yellow eyes and slightly smaller size.

Interesting Fact: North America's smallest owl.

North American Distribution and Habitat: An insectivorous migratory owl that breeds at the extreme eastern edge of California and southern Nevada through southern Arizona, southwestern New Mexico, and southern Texas. Winters in Mexico and Central America.

Nesting: Early March through mid-July, in woodpecker cavities in saguaros, trees, snags, agave stalks, and utility poles. Desert populations lay 2 to 5 eggs, canyon populations lay 1 to 4 eggs.

Vocalization: Rapid, descending *pe, pe, pe, pe, pe, pe.*

BURROWING OWL *(Athene cunicularia)*

Description: A small brown owl with long, unfeathered legs and flat head, approximately 9.5 inches long with a wingspan of 21 inches.

Similar Species: Unlikely to be confused with any other North American species.

Interesting Fact: The only owl to nest in loose colonies.

North American Distribution and Habitat: A year-round resident of grasslands and shrub-steppe areas of North America, east and south of the western mountains and in Florida.

Nesting: Mid-March through August, in the burrows of small mammals and in artificial burrows. Lays 1 to 11 eggs.

Vocalization: Double-note, single-pitched *cooo coooo* sung by male.

FLAMMULATED OWL *(Otus flammeolus)*

Description: A small reddish gray owl with black eyes, approximately 6.75 inches long with a wingspan of 16 inches. Can weigh less than 2 ounces.

Similar Species: Distinguished from Elf Owl by black eyes, slightly larger size, and ear tufts when in its cryptic posture.

Interesting Fact: The most migratory North American owl.

North American Distribution and Habitat: An insectivorous migratory owl that breeds in mountain pine forests throughout the West from south-central British Columbia to California, Arizona, and New Mexico. Winters south of the United States in Mexico and Central America.

Nesting: Early March through mid-August, in woodpecker cavities in trees and snags. Lays 2 to 4 eggs.

Vocalization: A flat tonal *hoot*.

EASTERN SCREECH-OWL *(Otus asio)*

Description: A small gray, brown, or red-eared owl with yellow eyes, approximately 8.5 inches long with a wingspan of 20 inches.

Similar Species: Distinguished from Western Screech-Owl mostly by call, although bill color also differs. Distinguished from Whiskered Screech-Owl by call and larger size.

Interesting Fact: Several color morphs exist, including a red morph most commonly found in moist, cloudy areas.

North American Distribution and Habitat: A resident owl in most of the eastern United States and a few parts of southern Canada.

Nesting: Early March through early September, in woodpecker cavities, nest boxes, and natural cavities in trees and snags predominantly in deciduous and mixed woods. Lays 2 to 6 eggs. Frequently reuses nest cavity.

Vocalization: A monotonic whistled trill.

WESTERN SCREECH-OWL *(Otus kennicottii)*

Description: A small gray, brown, or reddish eared owl with yellow eyes, approximately 8.5 inches long with a wingspan of 20 inches.

Similar Species: Distinguished from Eastern Screech-Owl mostly by call, although bill color also differs. Distinguished from Whiskered Screech-Owl by call and larger size.

Interesting Fact: Color varies regionally with lightest gray-colored birds in the driest habitats.

North American Distribution and Habitat: A resident owl south from southeast Alaska, west of the Rockies, and south to California, Arizona, New Mexico, and west Texas.

Nesting: Early May through June, in woodpecker cavities, nest boxes, and natural cavities in trees and snags, predominantly in deciduous and mixed woods. Lays 2 to 7 eggs. Often reuses nest cavities.

Vocalization: "Bouncing ball" call best described as a series of 5 to 9 or 9 to 15 short, whistled *hoots* becoming more tightly spaced toward their conclusion.

WHISKERED SCREECH-OWL *(Otus trichopsis)*

Description: A small grayish owl with ear tufts and gold orange eyes, approximately 7.25 inches long with a wingspan of 17.5 inches.

Similar Species: Distinguished from Eastern and Western Screech-Owls by smaller size and call.

Interesting Fact: Most limited U.S. distribution of any North American owl.

North American Distribution and Habitat: A Mexican Screech-Owl whose range enters the United States only in the mountains of southeast Arizona and southwest New Mexico.

Nesting: Early May until early August, in woodpecker cavities and natural cavities in trees and snags. Lays 3 to 4 eggs. Occasionally reuses nest cavity.

Vocalization: An evenly spaced group of several whistles.

FERRUGINOUS PYGMY-OWL *(Glaucidium brasilianum)*

Description: A small reddish brown owl, with a long tail, approximately 6.75 inches long with a wingspan of 12 inches.

Similar Species: More reddish brown compared to the darker brown of the Northern Pygmy-Owl, with tail bars of reddish brown rather than white. Streaked crown in contrast to the spotted crown of the Northern Pygmy-Owl.

Interesting Fact: Aggressive hunter, will take birds larger than itself.

North American Distribution and Habitat: A resident owl in south-central Arizona and southern Texas.

Nesting: Mid-April through late July, in woodpecker cavities in cacti or trees, or in natural cavities or nest boxes. Lays 2 to 7 eggs. Frequently reuses nest cavity.

Vocalization: A series of a few to a hundred evenly spaced notes prior to a pause.

NORTHERN PYGMY-OWL *(Glaucidium gnoma)*

Description: A small grayish brown or reddish brown owl, with a long tail, approximately 6.75 inches long with a wingspan of 12 inches.

Similar Species: In general, browner than the Ferruginous Pygmy-Owl, with tail bars of white rather than reddish as in the Ferruginous Pygmy-Owl. The crown is spotted in contrast to the Ferruginous Pygmy-Owl that has a streaked crown.

Interesting Fact: Like the Ferruginous Pygmy-Owl has false eyes on the back of head thought to ward off potential predators. An aggressive hunter, indifferent to human presence.

North American Distribution and Habitat: A resident owl in mixed forests of the West, from southeast Alaska to Arizona and New Mexico.

Nesting: Early April through late June, in woodpecker and natural cavities in trees or snags. Lays 2 to 7 eggs.

Vocalization: 1 or 2 hollow *toots* with a second or two between each.

WOODPECKERS

North America is home to 22 woodpeckers all belonging to the *Picadae* family and includes members of 5 genera. Among the genera are the *Melanerpes*, omnivorous woodpeckers that eat a variety of food including insects, fruit, and vertebrates such as lizards and frogs; *Sphyrapicus*, the sapsuckers, that drill sap wells in trees to consume sap and the insects attracted to the sap as a primary part of their diet; *Picoides*, which pursue insects on trees; *Colaptes*, ant specialists that often pursue their prey on the ground; and one member of the *Dryocopus* genus, a group of large woodpeckers with strong bills that excavate giant feeding cavities. All woodpeckers are diurnal birds that nest in cavities they create, usually in trees. Physically, woodpeckers vary in length from 6.75 inches to 16.5 inches from top of head to tip of tail. They breed in a variety of habitats that contain trees, large shrubs, or cacti, from high-elevation burns to low-lying deserts to the edge of the tree line in Alaska and Canada. Many are sedentary, several are migratory, and others are irruptive.

RED-HEADED WOODPECKER *(Melanerpes erythrocephalus)*

Description: A distinctive red-headed, medium-size woodpecker, approximately 9.25 inches long with a wingspan of 17 inches.

Similar Species: Unlikely to be confused with any other North American species.

Interesting Fact: Unpredictable distribution during winter when it wanders in search of nuts and acorns.

North American Distribution and Habitat: Occurs throughout much of the eastern United States outside of New England and the southern tip of Florida.

Nesting: Early May until early September. Often return to the same tree in consecutive years. Lays 3 to 10 eggs, although 4 to 7 is most common. Sometimes raise a second and less commonly a third brood in a single year.

Vocalization: *Tchurr, tchurr,* with each vocalization lasting less than half a second.

ACORN WOODPECKER *(Melanerpes formicivorus)*

Description: A medium-size woodpecker, approximately 9 inches long with a wingspan of 17.5 inches.

Similar Species: Unlikely to be confused with any other North American species.

Interesting Fact: Cooperative breeders.

North American Distribution and Habitat: Occurs in association with oaks in western North America in two disjunct populations: a small isolated population from extreme south-central Washington along the West Coast to southern California, and from central Arizona east to western New Mexico and south to Mexico.

Nesting: Mid-March through September. Cooperative group broods 2 to 8 eggs. Excavates its own cavities in whatever large trees are available, including telephone poles.

Vocalization: *Waka, waka, waka.*

LEWIS'S WOODPECKER *(Melanerpes lewis)*

Description: A colorful, large woodpecker, approximately 10.75 inches long with a wingspan of 21 inches.

Similar Species: Unlikely to be confused with any other North American species.

Interesting Fact: Often seen fly-catching (capturing insects on the wing) from elevated perches.

North American Distribution and Habitat: Occurs throughout much of the western United States, where it is often associated with ponderosa pine and pine-oak habitats.

Nesting: Late April through September. A weak excavator that sometimes returns to the same cavity to nest in consecutive years. Lays 5 to 9 eggs.

Vocalization: *Churr,* lasting roughly a half second and given a few to several times in succession.

GOLDEN-FRONTED WOODPECKER *(Melanerpes aurifrons)*

Description: A medium-size zebra-backed woodpecker, approximately 9.5 inches long with a wingspan of 17 inches.

Similar Species: Looks very similar and is closely related to both the Gila Woodpecker and the Red-bellied Woodpecker. Male features a red crown. Both sexes sport a yellowish nape.

Interesting Fact: One of two woodpeckers in North America that is expanding its range.

North American Distribution and Habitat: Breeds in arid brushlands and semi-open woodlands from southern Texas north into southwestern Oklahoma.

Nesting: Mid-March through July. Often reuses cavities. Lays 4 to 7 eggs. Second broods are common.

Vocalization: A loud, harsh *krrrr* that lasts less than half a second. During breeding season, 1 to 4 taps are followed by a series of rolling drums.

GILA WOODPECKER *(Melanerpes uropygialis)*

Description: A medium-size zebra-backed woodpecker, approximately 9.25 inches long with a wingspan of 16 inches.

Similar Species: Very similar in appearance and closely related to both the Golden-fronted Woodpecker and the Red-bellied Woodpecker. Male features a small red crown.

Interesting Fact: Eats the fruits of cacti, flowers, small animals, insects, and bird eggs.

North American Distribution and Habitat: Occurs in the arid parts of extreme southeastern California, southern Arizona, and extreme southwestern New Mexico.

Nesting: April through August. One of two birds that excavate cavities in saguaro cacti. Lays 3 to 6 eggs. Occasionally raises a second brood.

Vocalization: A double *churr*, with each *churr* note lasting roughly one-quarter of a second.

RED-BELLIED WOODPECKER *(Melanerpes carolinus)*

Description: A medium-size zebra-backed woodpecker, approximately 9.25 inches long with a wingspan of 16 inches.

Similar Species: Looks very similar and is closely related to both the Gila Woodpecker and the Golden-fronted Woodpecker. Both sexes feature a red nape; males also possess a red cap.

Interesting Fact: Extremely omnivorous, eating a wide variety of foods, including lizards and even frogs. Is expanding its range at a faster rate than any other woodpecker.

North American Distribution and Habitat: Breeds in a wide range of habitats throughout most of the eastern United States, where it is the most common woodpecker throughout much of the southern part of its range.

Nesting: Mid-April through mid-September. Red-bellied Woodpeckers commonly return to the same snag or dead limb to excavate a new cavity. Lays 3 to 6 eggs. Typically breeds once but may raise two or even three broods in southern part of its range.

Vocalization: A nearly half-second-long *kwirrr*.

WILLIAMSON'S SAPSUCKER *(Sphyrapicus thyroideus)*

Description: A medium-size woodpecker, approximately 9 inches long with a wingspan of 17 inches.

Similar Species: Adult males are unlikely to be confused with any other North American species, although adult females could be confused with juvenile Red-breasted, Red-naped, or Yellow-bellied Sapsuckers.

Interesting Fact: Male and female quite different in appearance, once considered separate species.

North American Distribution and Habitat: Occurs in mixed conifer forests throughout the western mountains, mostly in the United States. Two subspecies: *S.t. thyroideus* (western part of range) and *S.t. nataliae* (eastern part of range).

Nesting: Late April through late July. Often nests in the same snag. Lays 3 to 7 eggs.

Vocalization: Several consecutive *cheeur* notes.

RED-NAPED SAPSUCKER (*Sphyrapicus nuchalis*)

Description: A medium-size woodpecker, approximately 8.5 inches long with a wingspan of 16 inches.

Similar Species: Red-naped, Red-breasted, and Yellow-bellied Sapsuckers were considered regional variants of the same species until 1983. Red-naped lacks red head of Red-breasted yet has more red than Yellow-bellied, usually including some red on its nape.

Interesting Fact: Like other sapsuckers, creates sap wells in trees that are used by other animals, including several birds, for food.

North American Distribution and Habitat: Occurs in mountain forests of western North America.

Nesting: Mid-March through early August. Often nests in the same snag or aspen, sometimes in the same cavity. Lays 4 to 7 eggs.

Vocalization: Catlike mewing *keeah.*

RED-BREASTED SAPSUCKER (*Sphyrapicus ruber*)

Description: A medium-size woodpecker, approximately 8.5 inches long with a wingspan of 16 inches.

Similar Species: Red-breasted, Red-naped, and Yellow-bellied Sapsuckers were considered regional variants of the same species until 1983. The Red-breasted is distinguished by its mostly red head, particularly in the northern part of its range.

Interesting Fact: Like other sapsuckers, creates sap wells in trees that are used by other animals, including several birds, for food. Usually selects trees previously damaged or with previously drilled sap wells.

North American Distribution and Habitat: Occurs in forests along the west coast of North America, from southeast Alaska through southern California.

Nesting: Early March through July. Often nests again in the same snag or aspen. Lays 4 to 7 eggs.

Vocalization: Catlike mewing *keeah.*

YELLOW-BELLIED SAPSUCKER (*Sphyrapicus varius*)

Description: A medium-size woodpecker, approximately 8.5 inches long with a wingspan of 16 inches.

Similar Species: Yellow-bellied, Red-breasted, and Red-naped Sapsuckers were considered regional variants of the same species until 1983. The Yellow-bellied lacks the red head of the Red-breasted and the red nape of the Red-naped Sapsucker. Has the least red and the most white of the three.

Interesting Fact: Like other sapsuckers, creates tree sap wells that are used by other animals, including ruby-throated hummingbirds, which may rely on its wells upon arrival at breeding grounds.

North American Distribution and Habitat: Occurs throughout eastern North America and much of the boreal forest area.

Nesting: Early March through mid-July. Often nests again in the same snag or aspen and sometimes in the same cavity. Lays 2 to 7 eggs.

Vocalization: Catlike mewing *keeah.*

WHITE-HEADED WOODPECKER (*Picoides albolarvatus*)

Description: A medium-size white-headed woodpecker, approximately 9.25 inches long with a wingspan of 16 inches.

Similar Species: North America's only black-bodied bird with a white head.

Interesting Fact: North America's most pine nut-specialized woodpecker.

North American Distribution and Habitat: Occurs in mountain pine forests from southeastern British Columbia to Oregon, Idaho, California, and Nevada.

Nesting: Late April through mid-August. Excavates a cavity in large conifers (usually dead). Lays 4 to 5 eggs.

Vocalization: *Peek-ik.*

BLACK-BACKED WOODPECKER (*Picoides arcticus*)

Description: A medium-size black and white woodpecker, approximately 9.5 inches long with a wingspan of 16 inches.

Similar Species: The Three-toed Woodpecker looks quite similar but is smaller with more white. The Black-backed Woodpecker has a solid black back and a more solid yellow crown.

Interesting Fact: The Black-backed Woodpecker is a specialist of recently burned areas.

North American Distribution and Habitat: Primarily a boreal species, it can also be found in mid-elevation to subalpine habitats in the Cascades, Sierras, and northern Rockies; absent from the southern Rockies.

Nesting: Late May through late August. Nests in live trees or snags. Lays 2 to 6 eggs.

Vocalization: *Kyik* call sounds very similar to the Hairy Woodpecker; also uses a distinctive three-part *scream-rattle-snarl* call.

THREE-TOED WOODPECKER *(Picoides tridactylus)*

Description: A medium-size black and white woodpecker, approximately 8.75 inches long with a wingspan of 15 inches.

Similar Species: The Black-backed Woodpecker looks quite similar but is larger with more black. The Three-toed has white on its back and a less solid crown.

Interesting Fact: One of two North American woodpeckers that specializes in dead or diseased trees.

North American Distribution and Habitat: Primarily a boreal species, it ranges farther north than any other woodpecker and also extends into the spruce forests of the Cascades and Rockies.

Nesting: Mid-May through July. Nests in live or recently dead trees or snags. Lays 3 to 7 eggs.

Vocalization: *Kik* call given on its own or in a series, similar to Downy Woodpecker's call.

ARIZONA WOODPECKER *(Picoides arizonae)*

Description: A medium-size brown-backed woodpecker, approximately 7.5 inches long with a wingspan of 14 inches. Male has red feathers at the back of his crown.

Similar Species: Not likely to be confused with any other woodpecker.

Interesting Fact: North America's only brown-backed woodpecker.

North American Distribution and Habitat: Occurs in oak woods in the mountains of southeastern Arizona and southwestern New Mexico.

Nesting: Mid-April through late June. Excavates a cavity in a tree (usually dead). Lays 2 to 4 eggs.

Vocalization: A long *peep.*

RED-COCKADED WOODPECKER *(Picoides borealis)*

Description: A medium-size black-and-white woodpecker, approximately 8.5 inches long with a wingspan of 14 inches. Its red "cockade" consists of a few rarely seen red feathers on the head of the male.

Similar Species: Looks superficially like both the Ladder-backed and Nuttall's Woodpeckers, with completely white cheeks compared to their black eye stripes.

Interesting Fact: A cooperative breeder that lives in family groups.

North American Distribution and Habitat: Occurs sporadically in mature pine habitat, particularly longleaf pine, throughout the southeastern United States.

Nesting: Early April through July. Nests in mature live pine trees. Lays 2 to 5 eggs.

Vocalization: *Chirt* is the primary call note, given at intervals between 2 and 4 seconds.

NUTTALL'S WOODPECKER *(Picoides nuttallii)*

Description: A small zebra-backed, black-and-white woodpecker, approximately 7.5 inches long with a wingspan of 13 inches.

Similar Species: Resembles the closely related Ladder-backed Woodpecker but slightly larger with less red on the head and no barring on the upper part of the back.

Interesting Fact: An acrobatic woodpecker; frequently feeds while hanging from small twigs or berry clusters.

North American Distribution and Habitat: Occurs in oak habitat throughout much of California.

Nesting: Early April through mid-July. Excavates a cavity in extremely soft wood of decayed trunk or limb. Lays 3 to 6 eggs.

Vocalization: A high-pitched *pit* or *pitick.*

LADDER-BACKED WOODPECKER *(Picoides scalaris)*

Description: A small zebra-backed black-and-white woodpecker, approximately 7.25 inches long with a wingspan of 13 inches.

Similar Species: Resembles the closely related Nuttall's Woodpecker but is slightly smaller with more red on the head and barring that extends to the upper part of the back.

Interesting Fact: A nimble woodpecker that frequently feeds from the surface of cactus, trees, and shrubs.

North American Distribution and Habitat: Occurs throughout the arid landscapes of southeastern California, southern Nevada, and much of Arizona, New Mexico, and Texas.

Nesting: Mid-April through late July. Excavates a cavity in a tree, agave stalk, utility pole, or fence post. Lays 4 to 7 eggs.

Vocalization: *Peek* call similar to the Nuttall's but louder and higher in pitch.

DOWNY WOODPECKER *(Picoides pubescens)*

Description: A small black-and-white woodpecker, approximately 6.75 inches long with a wingspan of 12 inches.

Similar Species: Hairy Woodpecker is very similar in appearance, with a similar distribution, but the Downy is smaller with a proportionally smaller bill that is shorter than the length of its head.

Interesting Fact: Smallest woodpecker in North America.

North American Distribution and Habitat: One of the most widespread woodpeckers, breeding in deciduous and mixed habitats from near the tree line in Canada to the southern tip of Florida.

Nesting: Early April until late July. Usually nests in a dead tree or dead part of a living tree. Lays 3 to 8 eggs.

Vocalization: Simple *pik* calls, given alone or in a series, at a higher pitch than the similar call of the Hairy Woodpecker.

HAIRY WOODPECKER *(Picoides villosus)*

Description: A medium-size black-and-white woodpecker, approximately 9.25 inches long with a wingspan of 15 inches.

Similar Species: Very similar in appearance to Downy Woodpecker, and has a similar distribution; Hairy is larger, with a bill that is longer than the length of its head and a more chisel-shaped bill.

Interesting Fact: Plumage varies regionally, with the whitest individuals on the East Coast and sootier ones in the Pacific Northwest.

North American Distribution and Habitat: One of the most widespread woodpeckers, breeding in coniferous forests from near the tree line in Canada to the southern tip of Florida.

Nesting: Mid-March through July. Usually nests in a live tree with fungal rot. Lays 3 to 7 eggs.

Vocalization: Monosyllabic *peek* at a lower pitch than the similar call of the Downy Woodpecker.

NORTHERN FLICKER *(Colaptes auratus)*

Description: A large, distinctive brown woodpecker, 12.5 inches long on average with a wingspan of approximately 20 inches. A distinctive white rump patch is displayed in flight.

Similar Species: Similar to the Gilded Flicker but larger. Neither Red-shafted nor Yellow-shafted subspecies has brown nape, and both quite different from each other in appearance.

Interesting Fact: Often forages on the ground, where it specializes in ants.

North American Distribution and Habitat: Occurs throughout much of North America from tree line to southern Florida, except in the Sonoran Desert, where it is replaced by the Gilded Flicker, and in the arid landscape of much of Texas and southwestern New Mexico.

Nesting: Late April through early August. Excavates a cavity in dead or diseased trees. Lays 3 to 12 eggs.

Vocalization: A long series consisting of repeated *wik-a, wik-a, wik-a*, similar but lower in pitch than the Gilded Flicker.

GILDED FLICKER *(Colaptes chrysoides)*

Description: A large, distinctive brown woodpecker, approximately 11 inches long with a wingspan of 18 inches.

Similar Species: Similar to the Northern Flicker but smaller and with an all-brown crown and nape in contrast to the gray nape on the Northern Flicker (both Red-shafted and Yellow-shafted).

Interesting Fact: One of two North American woodpeckers that excavate cavities in saguaro cacti.

North American Distribution and Habitat: Occurs in the Sonoran Desert area of southeast California and southern Arizona.

Nesting: Early March through mid-August. Excavates a cavity in saguaro cacti. Lays 3 to 5 eggs. Sometimes raises 3 broods per year.

Vocalization: Long series consisting of repeated *wik-a, wik-a, wik-a*, similar to but higher in pitch than the Northern Flicker.

PILEATED WOODPECKER *(Dryocopus pileatus)*

Description: A large black woodpecker with a distinctive red crest, approximately 16 inches long with a wingspan of 29 inches.

Similar Species: Unlikely to be confused with any living North American woodpecker, though it looks similar to the larger extinct Ivory-billed Woodpecker.

Interesting Fact: Largest woodpecker in North America.

North American Distribution and Habitat: Breeds throughout all of the eastern United States, the southern half of the boreal forest, the northern Rockies, and much of the West Coast, including the Cascades, Olympics, and Sierras.

Nesting: Early May through mid-July. Typically excavates a cavity in a dead tree. Lays 1 to 6 eggs. Often reuses nests as roost cavities but not as nests.

Vocalization: Most well-known call is an extended *kuk-kuk, kuk-kuk* that can be heard in jungle scenes of some old movies.

Bibliography

BOOKS

Agee, James K. *Fire Ecology of Pacific Northwest Forests.* Washington, DC: Island Press, 1996.

Alden, Peter, and Brian Cassie. *National Audubon Society Field Guide to New England.* New York: Knopf, 1998.

Alden, Peter, and Peter Friederici. *National Audubon Society Field Guide to the Southwestern States:* New York: Knopf, 1999.

Alden, Peter, and Fred Heath. *National Audubon Society Field Guide to California.* New York: Knopf, 1998.

Alden, Peter, and Gil Nelson. *National Audubon Society Field Guide to the Southeastern States.* New York: Knopf, 1999.

Alden, Peter, and Dennis Paulson. *National Audubon Society Field Guide to the Pacific Northwest.* New York: Knopf, 1998.

Backhouse, Frances, *Woodpeckers of North America.* Buffalo, NY: Firefly Books, 2005.

Brown, David E., ed., *A Classification of North American Biotic Communities.* Salt Lake City: University of Utah Press, 1998.

Cannings, Richard, and Sydney Cannings. *British Columbia: A Natural History.* Vancouver, BC: Greystone Books, 1996.

Corman, Troy E., and Cathryn Wise-Gervais. *Arizona Breeding Bird Atlas.* Albuquerque: University of New Mexico Press, 2005.

Cutright, Paul Russell. *Lewis & Clark: Pioneering Naturalists.* Lincoln: University of Nebraska Press, 1989.

Franklin, Jerry F., and C. T. Dyrness. *Natural Vegetation of Oregon and Washington.* Corvallis: Oregon State University Press, 1988.

Johnsgard, Paul A. *North American Owls,* 2nd ed. Washington, DC: Smithsonian Institution Press, 2002.

Moulton, Gary E. *The Lewis & Clark Journals—An American Epic of Discovery:* Abridged ed. Lincoln: University of Nebraska Press, 2003.

Short, Lester L. *Woodpeckers of the World.* Greenville: Delaware Museum of Natural History, 1982.

Sibley, David Allen. *The Sibley Guide to Birds.* New York: Knopf, 2001.

Stepniewski, Andrew. *The Birds of Yakima County, Washington.* Yakima, WA: Yakima Valley Audubon Society, 1999.

Taylor, Richard Cachor. *A Birder's Guide to Southeastern Arizona.* Colorado Springs, CO: American Birding Association, 2005.

Voous, Karel H., *Owls of the Northern Hemisphere.* Cambridge, MA: MIT Press, 1988.

Wells, Jeffrey V. *Birder's Conservation Handbook: 100 North American Birds at Risk.* Princeton, NJ: Princeton University Press, 2007.

OTHER PUBLICATIONS

Aubry, Keith B., and Catherine M. Raley. *The Pileated Woodpecker as a Keystone Habitat Modifier in the Pacific Northwest.* USDA Forest Service General Technical Report PSW-GTR, 2002.

Blancher, Peter, and Jeffrey Wells. "The Boreal Forest Region: North America's Bird Nursery." (Ottowa, Canada: Canadian Boreal Initiative and Seattle, WA: Boreal Songbird Initiative, in conjunction: Bird Studies Canada, 2005), www.borealbirds.org /bsi-bscreport-april2005.pdf.

Butcher, Gregory S., and Daniel K. Niven. "Combining Data from the Christmas Bird Count and the Breeding Bird Survey to Determine the Continental Status and Trends of North American Birds." National Audubon Society, www.audubon.org/bird/stateofthebirds /cbid/content/Report.pdf.

Glick, Daniel. "Global Warming SOS." *Audubon* 109 (November–December 2007): 42–57.

Hayward, Gregory D., and Jon Verner, eds. *Flammulated, Boreal, and Great Gray Owls in the United States: A Technical Conservation Assessment.* USDA Forest Service, General Technical Report RM-253, September 1994.

Likhart, Brian D. "Home range and habitat of breeding Flammulated Owls in Colorado." *Wilson Bulletin,* September 1, 1998.

Martin, Kathy, Kathryn E. H. Aitken, and Karen Wiebe. "Nest Sites and Nest Webs for Cavity Nesting Communities in Interior British Columbia, Canada: Nest Characteristics and Niche Partitioning." *The Condor 106:5–19,* The Cooper Ornithological Society, 2004.

Wells, Jeff. "Buy for Birds Is an Idea with Wings." *Seattle Post-Intelligencer,* November 6, 2007, B7.

Poole, A., and F. Gill, eds. *The Birds of North America*. Philadelphia: Academy of Natural Sciences, and Washington, DC: American Ornithologists' Union. An invaluable resource, this series includes the following individual "life histories":

Bull, Evelyn L. and James R. Duncan. 1993. *Great Gray Owl (Strix nebulosa)*.

Bull, Evelyn L. and Jerome A. Jackson. 1995. *Pileated Woodpecker (Dryocopus pileatus)*.

Cannings, Richard J. and Tony Angell. 2001. *Western Screech-Owl (Megascops kennicottii)*.

Dixon, Rita D. and Victoria A. Saab. 2000. *Black-backed Woodpecker (Picoides arcticus)*.

Dobbs, R. C., T. E. Martin and C. J. Conway. 1997. *Williamson's Sapsucker (Sphyrapicus thyroideus)*.

Duncan, James R. and Patricia A. Duncan. 1998. *Northern Hawk Owl (Surnia ulula)*.

Edwards, Holly H. and Gary D. Schnell. 2000. *Gila Woodpecker (Melanerpes uropygialis)*.

Garrett, Kimball L., Martin G. Raphael and Rita D. Dixaon. 1996. *White-headed Woodpecker (Picoides albolarvatus)*.

Gehlbach, Frederick R. 1995. *Eastern Screech-Owl (Megascops asio)*.

Gehlbach, Frederick R. and Nancy Y. Gehlbach. 2000. *Whiskered Screech-Owl (Megascops trichopsis)*.

Gutiérrez, R. J., A. B. Franklin and W. S. Lahaye. 1995. *Spotted Owl (Strix occidentalis)*.

Haug, E. A., B. A. Millsap and M. S. Martell. 1993. *Burrowing Owl (Athene cunicularia)*.

Hayward, G. D. and P. H. Hayward. 1993. *Boreal Owl (Aegolius funereus)*.

Henry, Susanna G. and Frederick R. Gehlbach. 1999. *Elf Owl (Micrathene whitneyi)*.

Holt, Denver W. and Julie L. Petersen. 2000. *Northern Pygmy-Owl (Glaucidium gnoma)*.

Houston, C. Stuart, Dwight G. Smith and Christoph Rohner. 1998. *Great Horned Owl (Bubo virginianus)*.

Husak, Michael S. and Terry C. Maxwell. 1998. *Golden-fronted Woodpecker (Melanerpes aurifrons)*.

Jackson, Jerome A. 1994. *Red-cockaded Woodpecker (Picoides borealis)*.

Jackson, Jerome A. and Henri R. Ouellet. 2002. *Downy Woodpecker (Picoides pubescens)*.

Jackson, Jerome A., Henri R. Ouellet and Bette J. Jackson. 2002. *Hairy Woodpecker (Picoides villosus)*.

Johnson, R. Roy, Lois T. Haight and J. David Ligon. 1999. *Arizona Woodpecker (Picoides arizonae)*.

Koenig, Walter D., Peter B. Stacey, Mark T. Stanback and Ronald L. Mumme. 1995. *Acorn Woodpecker (Melanerpes formicivorus)*.

Leonard, Jr., David L. 2001. *American Three-toed Woodpecker (Picoides dorsalis)*.

Lowther, Peter E. 2000. *Nuttall's Woodpecker (Picoides nuttallii)*.

———. 2001. *Ladder-backed Woodpecker (Picoides scalaris)*.

Marks, J. S., D. L. Evans and D. W. Holt. 1994. *Long-eared Owl (Asio otus)*.

Marti, Carl D., Alan F. Poole and L. R. Bevier. 2005. *Barn Owl (Tyto alba)*.

Mazur, Kurt M. and Paul C. James. 2000. *Barred Owl (Strix varia)*.

Mccallum, D. Archibald. 1994. *Flammulated Owl (Otus flammeolus)*.

Moore, William S. 1995. *Gilded Flicker (Colaptes chrysoides), Northern Flicker (Colaptes auratus)*.

Parmelee, David F. 1992. *Snowy Owl (Bubo scandiacus)*.

Proudfoot, Glenn A. and R. Roy Johnson. 2000. *Ferruginous Pygmy-Owl (Glaucidium brasilianum)*.

Rasmussen, Justin Lee, Spencer Sealy and Richard J. Cannings. 2008. *Northern Saw-whet Owl (Aegolius acadicus)*.

Shackelford, Clifford E., Raymond E. Brown and Richard N. Conner. 2000. *Red-bellied Woodpecker (Melanerpes carolinus)*.

Smith, Kimberly G., James H. Withgott and Paul G. Rodewald. 2000. *Red-headed Woodpecker (Melanerpes erythrocephalus)*.

Tobalske, Bret W. 1997. *Lewis's Woodpecker (Melanerpes lewis)*.

Walters, Eric L., Edward H. Miller and Peter E. Lowther. 2002. *Red-breasted Sapsucker (Sphyrapicus ruber)*.

———. 2002. *Red-naped Sapsucker (Sphyrapicus nuchalis)*.

———. 2002. *Yellow-bellied Sapsucker (Sphyrapicus varius)*.

Wiggins, D. A., D. W. Holt and S. M. Leasure. 2006. *Short-eared Owl (Asio flammeus)*.

A Note About the Photography

All but one of the photographs in this book were taken with Canon digital cameras, including the 20D, 1D Mark II, and 1D Mark III. The majority of the bird images were made with the Canon 500mm f4 lens or the Canon 600mm f4 lens, often with a 1.4 multiplier attached. The Canon 300mm f4 and the Canon 70–200mm f2.8 were also used for birds, and the Canon 24–70mm f2.8 was used for some of the habitat photographs. A Gitzo 1325 tripod was used to support the camera and lenses for most of the photographs, and larger lenses were supported using a Wimberly head.

All images in this book are of wild subjects. None of the birds were captive or restrained in any way, although a few of the images feature fledgling owls that were moved by researchers during the banding process.

All photographs in this book are faithful documentations of the natural moments that I witnessed, including imperfections of the subject, background, and foreground. As with all professional-level digital photographs, the "raw" files have been processed to more accurately reflect the actual moment. The

A male Yellow-shafted Northern Flicker carries waste materials from the nest.

processing was limited almost exclusively to the conversion of "raw" to "TIFF," cropping, and the global application of levels, curves, saturation, and sharpening tools.

About the Author

Wildlife, nature, and bird photographer Paul Bannick strives to capture images that foster a sense of intimacy with the subject. His work has been widely published in books and magazines, as well as used in displays in parks, natural areas, and institutions throughout North America. As an experienced naturalist, outdoorsman, and outdoor educator, Paul creates many of his images while hiking, kayaking, and snowshoeing throughout the world.

After graduating from the University of Washington, Paul worked for fifteen years in the computer software industry, initially as one of the original seventy-five employees of the Aldus Corporation, and then for Adobe Systems and Microsoft. He left the software industry in 2001 to work full-time for non-profit conservation organizations that are dedicated to protecting habitat and recovering species. More of Paul's work can be seen at www.paulbannick.com.

Index

THE MOUNTAINEERS, founded in 1906, is a nonprofit outdoor activity and conservation club, whose mission is "to explore, study, preserve, and enjoy the natural beauty of the outdoors. . . ." Based in Seattle, Washington, the club is now the third-largest such organization in the United States, with seven branches throughout Washington State.

The Mountaineers sponsors both classes and year-round outdoor activities in the Pacific Northwest, which include hiking, mountain climbing, ski-touring, snowshoeing, bicycling, camping, kayaking, nature study, sailing, and adventure travel. The club's conservation division supports environmental causes through educational activities, sponsoring legislation, and presenting informational programs.

All club activities are led by skilled, experienced instructors, who are dedicated to promoting safe and responsible enjoyment and preservation of the outdoors.

If you would like to participate in these organized outdoor activities or the club's programs, consider a membership in The Mountaineers. For information and an application, write or call The Mountaineers, Club Headquarters, 300 Third Avenue West, Seattle, WA 98119; 206-284-6310. You can also visit the club's website at www.mountaineers.org or contact The Mountaineers via email at clubmail@mountaineers.org.

The Mountaineers Books, an active, nonprofit publishing program of the club, produces guidebooks, instructional texts, historical works, natural history guides, and works on environmental conservation. All books produced by The Mountaineers Books fulfill the club's mission.

Send or call for our catalog of more than 500 outdoor titles:

The Mountaineers Books
1001 SW Klickitat Way, Suite 201
Seattle, WA 98134
800-553-4453
mbooks@mountaineersbooks.org
www.mountaineersbooks.org